The Tale of Thorstein Staff-Struck

Original Text, Translations, and Word Lists

Translated by
Matthew Leigh Embleton

Copyright ©2025 Matthew Leigh Embleton. All rights reserved.

The Tale of Thorstein Staff-Struck

The Tale of Thorstein Staff-Struck (*Old Norse*) 4
Word List *(Old Norse to English)* 24
Word List *(English to Old Norse)* 36
The Tale of Thorstein Staff-Struck (*Old Icelandic*) 46
Word List *(Old Icelandic to English)* 65
Word List *(English to Old Icelandic)* 76
A Word Comparison of Old Norse and Old Icelandic Words 86

Cover: Old Norse text over an outline of Iceland. Author's design.

The original Old Norse and Old Icelandic texts are in the public domain.
These translations ©2022 Matthew Leigh Embleton
©2025 Matthew Leigh Embleton (This Edition)

Acknowledgments

I have long been fascinated by languages and history, and I am very grateful to the special people in my life who have supported and encouraged me in my work. Thank you for believing in me. You know who you are.

Introduction

Old Norse is a North Germanic language spoken by inhabitants of Scandinavia from about the 7th to the 15th centuries. Old Icelandic is a variety of Old West Norse that emerged during the Norse settlement of Iceland in the second half of the 9th century. The rich tradition of Icelandic literature survived by oral tradition over several centuries before being written down in the 13th Century. The Tale of Thorstein Staff-Struck (*Þórsteins þáttr stangarhöggs*) is one of the many Tales of Icelanders or *Íslendingaþættir*. The word '*þáttr*' (plural: '*þættir*') translates as a strand of rope or a yarn, comparable to the word 'yarn' in English sometimes used to refer to a story.

This book contains:
- The Tale of Thorstein Staff-Struck (*Þórsteins þáttr stangarhöggs*) (Old Norse Version)
- An Old Norse to English Word List
- An English to Old Norse Word List
- The Tale of Thorstein Staff-Struck (*Þórsteins þáttr stangarhöggs*) (Old Icelandic Version)
- An Old Icelandic to English Word List
- An English to Old Icelandic Word List
- A Word Comparison of Old Norse and Old Icelandic words

The texts are presented in their original form, with a literal word-for-word line-by-line translation, and a Modern English translation, all side-by-side. In this way, it is possible to see and feel how the worked and how it has evolved. This book is designed to be of use and interest to anyone with a passion for the Old Norse or Old Icelandic language, Norse history, or languages and history in general.

The Tale of Thorstein Staff-Struck (*Old Norse*)

Old Norse	Literal	English
1	**1**	**1**
Þórarinn hét maðr, er bjó í Sunnudal, gamall maðr ok sjónlitill.	Thorarin was-named a-man, who lived in Sunnudal, old man and seeing-little.	There was a man named Thorarin who lived in Sunnudal, he was an old man and nearly blind.
Hann hafði verit víkingr mikill í œsku sinni.	He had been viking great in youth his.	He had been a fierce viking in his youth.
Engi var hann dældarmaðr, þótt hann væri gamall.	None was he gentle-man, though he was old.	He was not a gentle man even though he was old.
Son átti hann einn, er Þórsteinn hét.	A-son had he one, who Thorstein was-named.	He had a son who was named Thorstein.
Hann var mikill maðr ok öflugr ok vel stiltr, ok vann svá fyrir búi föður síns, at eigi mundi þriggja manna annarra verk haldkvæmara.	He was great man and powerful and well composed, and worked so for estate father his, that not could three men other work hold-fulfil.	He was a great and powerful man and well composed, and he worked so hard on his father's estate that three other men could not fulfil.
Þórarinn var heldr félitill maðr, enn allmargt átti hann vápna.	Thorarin was rather fee-little man, then all-many had he weapons.	Thorarin was rather a poor man but he had many weapons.
Þeir áttu ok stóðhross feðgar, ok var þeim þat helzt til fjár, er þeir seldu undan hestana, því at engir brugðust at reið né dugi.	They had also stud-horses father-and-son, and was their that rather to fee, that they sold away horses, because that none broke that ride nor spirit.	They also had some stud horses and that was their main source of wealth, for the horses they sold were not broken by riding nor broken in spirit.
Þórðr er maðr nefndr;	Thord was a-man named;	There was a man named Thord.
hann var húskarl Bjarna frá Hofi.	he was servant Bjarni's from Hof.	He was a servant of Bjarni from Hof.
Hann varðveitti reiðhesta Bjarna; því var hann kallaðr Þórðr hrossamaðr.	He looked-after riding-horses Bjarni's; accordingly was he called Thord horse-man.	He looked after Bjarni's riding-horses and was therefore called horse-man.
Hann var ójafnaðar maðr mikill, ok lét marga þess kenna, at hann var riks manns húskarl;	He was un-equal-man man great, and had many this be-known, that he was noble man's servant;	Thord was very much an arrogant man and he had it known that he was a nobleman's servant.

The Tale of Thorstein Staff-Struck (Old Norse)

Old Norse	Literal	English
enn eigi var hann sjálfr at meira verðr, ok varð hann eigi at vinsælli.	but not was he himself that more worth, and was he not that popular.	But this did not add to his worth or his popularity.
Þeir menn váru enn á vist með Bjarna, er annarr hét Þórhallr enn annarr Þórvaldr.	They men were then in hospitality with Bjarni, who one named Thorhall and another Thorvald.	There were then men staying with Bjarni, one was named Thorhall, and another Thorvald.
Þeir váru uppaustrarmenn miklir um allt þat, er þeir heyrðu í heraðinu.	They were gossipers much about all that, which they heard in the-district.	They were very much gossipers about all that the heard in the district.
Þeir Þórsteinn ok Þórðr mæltu til hesta-ats ungum hestum,	They Thorstein and Thord spoke-of to horse-fight young horses,	Thorstein and Thord spoke about a horse fight for their young horses.
ok er þeir öttu þeim, vildi hestr Þórðar verr bítast.	and when they matched their, would horse Thord's worst bite.	And when they fought, Thord's horse was bitten the worst.
Þórðr lýstr nú á skoltinn hesti Þórsteins, er honum þótti sinn hestr verr hafa, mikit högg;	Thord struck now to jaw horse Thorstein's, when he thought his horse worse had, much been-struck;	Thord now struck the jaw of Thorstein's horse when he realised that his horse had been struck worse.
enn Þórsteinn sá þat, ok laust á móti best Þórðar heldr meira högg, ok rann nú hestr Þórðar, ok œptu menn nú með kappi.	then Thorstein saw that, and struck to towards the-horse Thord's rather more striking, and ran now horse Thord's, and called-out men now with warriors.	Then Thorstein saw that and struck at Thord's horse rather more, and Thord's horse backed away, and then the warriors who were with them called out.
Þá lýstr Þórðr Þórstein með hestastafnum, ok kom á brúnina, ok hljóp hon ofan fyrir augat.	Then struck Thord Thorstein with horse-staffs, and came to eyebrow, and ran it over before eye.	Then Thord struck Thorstein with his horse staff which came to his eyebrow and ran over his eye.
Þá reist Þórsteinn af skyrtublaði sínu ok batt upp brúnina, ok lætr sem eigi hafi at orðit, ok biðr menn leyna þessu föður hans,	Then carved Thorstein off shirt-sheet his and bound up eyebrow, and behaved as-if not had that worded, and asked people keep-secret this father his,	Then Thorstein carved from his shirt and bandaged his eyebrow and behaved thus that he did not say anything about it, and he asked people to keep this a secret from his father.
ok fell þetta þar nú niðr.	and fell that there now down.	And the matter fell down there.

The Tale of Thorstein Staff-Struck (Old Norse)

Old Norse	Literal	English
Þeir Þórhallr ok Þórvaldr höfðu fyrir kals, ok kölluðu hann Þórstein stangarhögg.	They Thorhall and Thorvald had before taunted, and called him Thorstein Staff-Struck.	Thorvald and Thorhall has thus taunted him and called him Thorstein Staff-Struck.
Litlu fyrir jól um vetrinn rísa konur til verks í Sunnudal.	Little before Yule about winter rose women to work in Sunnudal.	A little before Yule in winter when women got up to work in Sunnudal.
Þá stóð Þórsteinn upp ok bar inn hey, ok lagðist síðan í bekk.	Then stood Thorstein got-up and carried in hay, and laid then on bench.	Then Thorstein got up and carried some hay inside and then lay down on a bench.
Nú kemr Þórarinn karl inn, faðir hans, ok spyrr, hverr þar lægi.	Now came Thorarin old-man in, father his, and asked, why there laying.	Now Thorarin his father, an old man, came in and asked him why he was laying there.
Þórsteinn segir til sín.	Thorstein said to him.	Thorstein told him.
"Hvi ertú svá snemma á fótum, sonr?"	"Why are-you so early about feet, son?"	"Why are you up on your feet so early, son?",
segir Þórarinn.	said Thorarin.	said Thorarin the old man.
Þórsteinn svarar:	Thorstein answered:	Thorstein answered:
"Við fá þykkir mér at meta þat er hér þarf at vinna".	"With few seems to-me to meet that which here needs that win".	"With few it seems to me that might help me here",
"Er þér ekki illt í höfuðbeinum, sonr?",	"Are you not ill in head-bone, son?",	"Are you not ill in the head, son?",
segir Þórarinn.	said Thorarin.	said the old man.
"Eigi kenni ek þess",	"Not know I this",	"Not that I have noticed",
segir Þórsteinn.	said Thorstein.	said Thorstein.
"Hvat segir þú mér, sonr", segir Þórarinn, "af hesta-þinginu, því er var í sumar? Vartú eigi lostinn í svima, frændi, sem hundr?"	"What say you to-me, son", said Thorarin, "off horse-fight, which that was in summer? Were-you not struck to dizziness, kinsmen, as a-dog?"	What can you tell me about the horse fight last summer? Were you not struck dizzy by your kinsmen like a dog?"
"Engi þykki mér svivirðing í vera",	"Nothing seems to-me worthy to be",	"It is not worthy to me",

The Tale of Thorstein Staff-Struck (Old Norse)

Old Norse	Literal	English
segir Þórsteinn, "at kalla þat heldr högg enn atburð".	said Thorstein, "to call that rather striking then accident".	said Thorstein, "to call it rather a blow than an incident".
Þórarinn mælti:	Thorarin said:	Thorarin said:
"Eigi mundi mik þess vara, at ek munda eiga ragan son".	"Not thought meet this would-be, that I would have cowardly a-son".	"Not would this be to me, that I would have a coward son".
"Mæl þú þat nú eitt um, faðir",	"Say you that now one-thing about, father",	"Tell me one thing about now, father",
segir Þórsteinn, "er þér þykkir eigi of mælt síðar".	said Thorstein, "that you seem not of speaking afterwards".	said Thorstein, "which you do not think is said-too-much later".
"Eigi man ek hér svá mikit um mæla",	"Not shall I here so much about speak",	"I will not speak so much here",
segir Þórarinn, "sem mér er at skapi".	said Thorarin, "as to-me is to mind".	said Thorarin, "of what I am in the mood to say".

2

Nú reis Þórsteinn upp ok tók vápn sín ok gekk heiman ok fór unz hann kom at hrossahúsi því, er Þórðr gætti hesta Bjarna, ok var hann þar fyrir.	Now rose Thorstein up and took weapon his and went home and travelled until he came to horse-house because, that Thord guarded horses Bjarni's, and was he there before.	Now Thorstein got up and took his weapon, and then went away from home, and went until he came to the horse-house where Thord looked after Bjarni's horses, and he was there before.
Þá hittir Þórsteinn Þórð, ok mælti til hans:	Then found Thorstein Thord, and spoke to him:	Then Thorstein met Thord, and said to him,
"Vita vilda ek þat, Þórðr, hvárt þat var váðaverk, er ek fekk af þér högg í sumar á hestaþingi, eðr hefir þat orðit at vilja þínum; mantú þá vilja bœta yfir".	"Know wish I that, Thord, whether that was accident, that I got of you a-strike in summer at horse-fight, or have that words that wish you; should then will compensation over".	"I wish to know, my Thord, whether it was a tragedy to you when I was beaten by you last summer at a horse meeting, or whether it has been at your will, and whether you will make amends for it".
Þórðr svarar:	Thord answered:	Thord answered:

The Tale of Thorstein Staff-Struck (Old Norse)

Old Norse	Literal	English
"Ef þú átt tvá hváftana, þá bregð þú tungunni sitt í hvárn, ok kalla í öðrum váðaverk, ef þú vilt; enn í öðrum kalla þú alvöru,	"If you had two mouths, then move you tongue yours in each, and call in the-other an-accident, if you wish; but in the-other call you seriously,	"If you had two mouths, then you could move your tongue into each and call it either an accident if you wish but in another call it serious.
ok eru þar svá miklar bœtrnur sem þú mant af mér fá".	and are-you there so much compensation as-if you shall of met get".	And now those are the benefits you'll get from me".
"Bústú þá svá við",	"Settle then so with",	"Settle with that as you will",
segir Þórsteinn,	said Thorstein,	said Thorstein,
"at "at vera má, at ek heimta eigi oftar".	"that to be, may that I claim not". often	"it may be that I don't make this claim often".
Síðan hleypr Þórsteinn at honum ok höggr hann banahögg; gekk síðan til húss at Hofi, ok hitti úti konu eina ok mælti við hana:	Then ran Thorstein at him and struck he death-blow; went afterwards to house at Hof, and met outside woman one and spoke with her:	Then Thorstein ran at him and stuck Thord his death-blow, and went afterwards to the house at Hof and met a woman outside and spoke with her:
"Seg þú Bjarna, at naut hafi stangat Þórð hestasvein hans, ok mun hann biða þar til þess, er hann kemr, hjá hesthúsinn".	"Tell you Bjarni, that bull had gored Thord horse-boy his, and should he abide there to this, that he comes, beside horse-house".	"Tell Bjarni that a bull has gored Thord horse-man, and he should wait there until he comes to the stable".
"Far þú heim maðr",	"Travel you home man",	"Go back home, man",
segir hon,	said she,	she said,
"enn ek segi þá er mér sýnist".	"then I say then what to-me seems".	"and I will way when it seems to me to do so".
Nú ferr Þórsteinn heim, en konan fór til verks síns.	Now travelled Thorstein home, and the-woman went to work hers.	Now Thorstein travelled home and the woman went to her work.

3

Bjarni reis upp um morguninn; ok er hann var kominn undir borð, þá spyrr hann, hvar Þórðr væri ok svöruðu menn, at hann mundi til hrossa farinn.	Bjarni rose up about morning; and as he was came under the-table, then asked he, where Thord was and answered people, that he would to the-horses gone.	Bjarni got up that morning and was sitting at the table, then Bjarni asked where Thord was, and people answered that he would have travelled to the horses.

The Tale of Thorstein Staff-Struck (Old Norse)

Old Norse	Literal	English
"Heim hugða ek hann þó mundu kominn",	"Home thought I he though would come",	"I thought he would have come home",
segir Bjarni,	said Bjarni,	said Bjarni,
"ef hann væri heill".	"if he was healthy".	"if he was well".
Þá tók kona til orða, sú er Þórsteinn hafði hitta:	Then took the-woman to words, that which Thorstein had met:	Then the woman that Thorsten had met took to words:
"Satt er þat, er oss er oft sagt konum, at þar er lítt til vits at taka, sem vér erum konur.	"True is that, which we are often told women, that there is little to wits to take, which we are women.	"It is true what is told of us women, that there is little to wits taken as we are women.
Hér kom Þórsteinn stangarhögg í morgun, ok kvað naut hafa stangat Þórð, svá at hann mundi eigi sjálfbjarga verða,	Here came Thorstein Staff-Struck in morning, and said a-bull had gored Thord, so it, that, to he could not self-supported be,	Thorstein Staff-Struck came here this morning, and said a bull had struck Thord so that he could not support himself.
enn ek nenta þá ekki at vekja þik, ok hvarf mér ór hug síðan".	but I wanted then not to wake you, and disappeared to-me from thoughts afterwards".	But I didn't want to wake you, and then it disappeared from my thoughts afterwards".
Bjarni sté þá undan borði, gekk til hrossahússins ok fann þar Þórð veginn; ok var hann síðan jarðaðr.	Bjarni stepped then from-under the-table, went to horse-house and found there Thord killed; and was he then earthed.	Bjarni stepped out from under the table, and then went to the stable and found Thord there killed, and he was buried afterwards.
Bjarni býr nú málit til þings ok gerir Þórstein sekan um vigit;	Bjarni prepared now a-case towards the-assembly and make Thorstein guilty about the-killing;	Bjarni now prepared a case to make Thorstein guilty of the killing.
enn Þórsteinn sat heima í Sunnudal, ok vann fyrir föður sínum, ok lét Bjarni þó kyrt vera.	then Thorstein sat home in Sunnudal, and worked for father his, and had Bjarni though still be.	But Thorstein stayed at home in Sunnudal and worked for his father, and Bjarni had little done though.
Um haustit sátu menn við sviðelda at Hofi, enn Bjarni lá úti á eldhúsveggnum, ok hlýddi þaðan til tals manna.	About autumn sat people with bonfires at Hof, when Bjarni lay out on fire-house-wall, and followed from there talk people's.	About autumn the people of Hof had bonfires, and Bjarni lay outside on the fire-house-wall and followed other people's talking.

The Tale of Thorstein Staff-Struck (Old Norse)

Old Norse	Literal	English
Nú taka þeir bræðr tíl orða, Þórhallr ok Þórvaldr, ok mæltu svá:	Now took they brothers to words, Thorhall and Thorvald, and spoke-of so:	Now the brothers Thorhall and Thorvald took to words:
"Eigi varði oss, þá er vér tókum vist með Víga-Bjarna, at vér mundum hér svíða dilka-höfuð, enn Þórsteinn skógarmaðr hans skyldi svíða geldinga-höfuð,	"Not expected us, then when we-are taking provisions with Killer-Bjarni, that we would here singe sheep-heads, then Thorstein outlaw his should singe ram-heads,	"We did not expect when we came to stay with Killer-Bjarni that we would be here singing sheeps" heads when Thorstein the outlaw would be singing rams' heads.
væri eigi verra, at hafa meirr vægt frændum sínum í Böðvarsdal, ok sæti nú eigi skógarmaðrinn jafnhátt honum í Sunnudal,	would not-be worse, than have more mercy kinsmen his in Bodvarsdale, and sat now not outlawed equally him in Sunnudal,	It would not have been worse to have his merciful kinsmen in Bodvarsdale and not sat equally with the outlaw in Sunnudal.
enn hinir verða forlagðir, er fyrir sárunum verða, ok vitum vér eigi, hvenær hann vill þenna flekk má af virðingu sinni".	then they became mislaid, who before injury comes, and know we not, when he will this stain may of worthiness his".	But what is laid becomes mislaid when it becomes faced with injury, and we don't know when he will off this stain from his honour".
Maðr einn svarar:	Man one answered:	One man answered:
"Slíkt er verr mælt enn þagat, oklíklegt, at yðr hafi troll togat tungu ör höfði;	"Such is worse spoken than silence, and-likely, that you have trolls pulled tongue out-of head;	"Such that is spoken is worse than silence, and it's likely that the trolls pulled the tongue out of your head.
ætlum vér, at hann nenni eigi at taka björg frá föður hans sjönlausum ok annarri ómegð þeiri sem er í Sunnudal.	#REF! we, that he bothers not to take help from father his sight-less and another without there as at in Sunnudal.	We think that he does not bother to take help from his blind father and other dependants there at Sunnudal.
Enn kynlegt þykki mér, ef þér sviðit oft lambahöfuðin hér, eðr hrósit því hvat títt var í Böðvarsdal".	Then surprised think I, if you-two singe often lambs-heads here, or praise therefore what reported was in Bodvarsdale".	But I will be surprised if you two singe many more lamb's heads here, or talk about what happened at Bodvarsdale".
Nú fara menn til borða ok síðan til svefns, ok fann eigi á Bjarna, hvat talat hafði verit.	Now travelled men to the-tables and then to sleep, and found not of Bjarni, what told had been.	Now the people went to the tables and then to sleep and Bjarni gave nothing away of what had been told.

The Tale of Thorstein Staff-Struck (Old Norse)

Old Norse	Literal	English
# 4	# 4	# 4
Um morguninn vakti Bjarni þá Þórhall ok Þórvald, ok bað þá fara í Sunnudal ok fœra sér höfuð Þórsteins við bolinn skilit at dagmálum.	About morning awoke Bjarni then Thorhall and Thorvald, and asked then to-travel to Sunnudal and travelled themselves head Thorstein's with torso divided that mid-morning.	About morning Bjarni woke Thorhall and Thorvald and asked them to ride to Sunnudal and bring Thorstein's severed head divided from its torso by mid-morning
"Ok þykki mér", segir hann, þit liklegastir til at fœra flekk af virðingu minni, er ek hefi eigi þrek til sjálfr".	"And seems to-me", said he, this likeliest to that bring stain of worthiness mine, when I have not strength to myself".	"and it seems to me that you", he said, "will bring the stain off my honour if I have not the strength to myself".
Nú þykkjast þeir víst ofmælt hafa, ok fara þeir nú þó, unz þeir koma í Sunnudal.	Now thought they knew said-too-much had, and travelled they now though, until they came to Sunnudal.	Now they thought that they had said too much, but they travelled until they came to Sunnudal.
Þórsteinn stóð í durum, ok hvatti sax;	Thorstein stood in doorway, and sharpened short-sword;	Thorstein stood in the doorway and sharpened a short-sword.
ok er þeir koma þar, þá spurði hann, hvert þeir ætluðu.	and as they came there, then asked he, what they intended.	And as they came he asked them what their intentions were,
Enn þeir kváðust hrossa leita skyldu.	Then they said horses looking-for should.	and they said that they were looking for some horses,
Enn Þórsteinn kvað þeira mundu skamt at leita, "er þau eru hér við garð".	Then Thorstein said they would short to look-for, "but they were here with fences".	then Thorstein said that they would not have to look far "but they are here by the fence".
"Eigi er víst at vit finnim hrossin, ef þú vísar okkr ekki til", segja þeir.	"Not is-it certain that with finding horses, if you refer us not to", tell they.	"It is not certain that we will find the horses if you do not refer us".
Þórsteinn gengr þá út,	Thorstein went then outside,	Then Thorstein went outside.
ok er þeir koma fyrir garðinu ofan, þá fœrir Þórvaldr upp öxina ok hleypr at honum; enn Þórsteinn stakk við honum hendi sinni, svá at hann fell fyrir.	and as they came before meadow across, then brought Thorvald up axe and ran at him; but Thorstein pushed against him arms his, so that he fell before.	And as they went across the meadow, Thorvald brought up an axe and ran at him but Thorstein pushed against his arms so that he fell before him.
Þórsteinn lágði saxinu í gegnum hann.	Thorstein laid short-sword in through him.	Thorstein laid his short-sword through him.

The Tale of Thorstein Staff-Struck (Old Norse)

Old Norse	Literal	English

Þá vildi Þórhallr veita honum tilræði ok hafði hann slika för sem Þórvaldr.

Then willed Thorhall to-give him assault and had he such for as Thorvald.

Then Thorhall wished to assault him, and he had the same as Thorvald.

Þá bindr Þórsteinn á bak báða þá, ok lætr upp taumana á hála hestunum, ok visar á leið öllu saman, ok ganga hestarnir nú heim til Hofs.

Then tied Thorstein to back both then, and had up reins to neck horses, and saw to pass all together, and went the-horses now home to Hof.

Then Thorstein tied both back and had the reins up to the horses necks and saw them off together, an the horses went home to Hof.

Húskarlar váru úti at Hofi, ok gengu inn ok segja Bjarna, at þeir Þórvaldr váru heim komnir, ok segja þá eigi erindislaust farit hafa.

Servants were out at Hof, and went in and told Bjarni, that they Thorvald were home coming, and told then not errand-lost gone had.

The servants were outside at Hof and went in and told Bjarni that Thorvald and Thorhall had come home, and said that their errand had not gone in vain.

Nú gengr Bjarni út, ok sér nú, hvernig um er búit, ok hefir ekki orð um.

Now went Bjarni out, and himself now, how about was prepared, and had not words about.

Now Bjarni went out himself about what had happened, and had no more words about it, and had them buried.

Lætr hann nú jarða þá, ok er nú kyrt allt, unz jól líðr.

Had he now buried then, and was now peace all, until Yule passed.

And it was now all peaceful until Yule had passed.

5

Þá tekr Rannveig til orða einn aftan, er þau koma í sæng sína, Bjarni ok hon:

Then took Rannveig to words one evening, when they came to bed theirs, Bjarni and her:

Then Rannveig spoke one evening when her and Bjarni came to their bed:

"Hvat ætlar þú at sé tiðast talat í heraðinu?";

"What suppose you that is news talking in the-district?";

"What do you suppose people are talking about in the district?"

segir hon.

said she.

she said.

"Eigi veit ek þat",

"Not know I that",

"I do not know",

segir Bjarni.

said Bjarni.

said Bjarni.

"Margir eru, at því er mér þykkir, ómjúkir í orðum sínum", segir hon;

"Many they-are, that therefore are to-me seeming, unremarkable in words theirs", said she;

"I think many of their words are unremarkable", he said.

The Tale of Thorstein Staff-Struck (Old Norse)

Old Norse	Literal	English
"ok er þat nú tíðast at rœða, at menn þykkjast eigi vita, hvat Þórsteinn stangarhögg muni þess gera, at þér muni þurfa þykkja at hefna;	"and is it now news that discussing, that people consider not known, what Thorstein Staff-Struck would this do, that you would need to-think to revenge;	"This is now what people are talking about, they think they don't know what Thorstein Staff-Struck would have to do for you to take revenge.
hefir hann nú vegit húskarla þína þrjá.	has he now killed servants yours three.	He has now killed three of your servants.
Þykkir þingmönnum þínum eigi vænt til halds, þar er þú ert, ef þessarra er óhefnt, ok eru þér mjök mislagðar hendr í kné".	Think assembly-men yours not expect to hold, there as you are, if this is without-revenge, and are you much misplaced hands on knees".	Your assembly-men do not expect to stay here as you are, if this is without revenge, and you have misplaced your hands on your knees.
Bjarni svarar:	Bjarni answered:	Bjarni answered:
"Hér kemr nú at því sem mælt er, at engi lætr sér annars víti at varnaði verða; enn hlýða mun ek þér, hvat er þú mælir;	"Here comes now that since which spoken is, that no-one has himself another's penalty to warn become; but listen should I to-you, what is you speak;	"Now it comes to what is said, that no one gives himself another's misfortune as a warning, but I will obey you what you say.
hefir Þórsteinn þá ok saklausa drepit".	has Thorstein then and without-cause killed".	Thorstein has killed few without cause".
Hætta þau þessu tali ok sofa af um nóttina.	Concluded then this talking and slept of about the-night.	Then their talking concluded and they slept through the night.
Um morguninn vaknar Rannveig, er Bjarni tók ofan skjöldinn, ok spurði hon, hvert hann skyldi.	About morning awoke Rannveig, as Bjarni took down shield, and asked her, which he should-be.	In the morning Rannveig woke up when Bjarni took down his shield and she asked where he was going.
Hann svarar:	He answered:	He answered:
"Nú skal skifta virðingu með okkr Þórsteini í Sunnudal",	"Now shall exchange honour between us Thorstein in Sunnudal",	"Now we shall exchange honour between us, Thorstein in Sunnudal",
segir hann.	said he.	he said.
"Hversu fjölmennr skaltú vera?"	"How-many followers shall be?"	"How many followers shall you travel with?",
segir hon.	said she.	she said.

The Tale of Thorstein Staff-Struck (Old Norse)

Old Norse	Literal	English
"Eigi mun ek draga fjölmenni at Þórsteini",	"Not shall I drag followers to Thorstein",	"I shall not drag followers to Thorstein",
segir hann,	said he,	he said,
"ok mun ek einn fara".	"and shall I one travelled".	"and I shall travel alone".
"Gerðú eigi þat",	"Do-you not that",	"Do not do that",
segir hon"	said she?"	she said,
"at hætta þér einum undir vápn heljarmannsins".	"to risk to-you one up-to weapons cursed-man-this".	"to risk yourself alone up against the weapons of this cursed man".
Bjarni mælti:	Bjarni spoke:	Bjarni spoke:
"Mun þér nú ekki verða þeira kvenna dœmi, er gráta á annarri stundu, er þær eggja á annarri? Enn ek þoli oft lengr frýju-orð bæði af þér ok öðrum; énn þá stoðar ok eigi at letja mik, er ek vil fara".	"Should you now not become those women judging, who-are weeping at another time, who there encouraging in another? But I tolerate often along taunting both of you and other; but then support and not to discourage me, as I wish to-go".	"Should you not now become one-of-those women who deem to weep at one moment but encourage at another? Before I have tolerated frequently and long enough the taunts of you and others, but then support me and not discourage me as I wish to go".
Bjarni fór nú í Sunnudal, ok stendr Þórsteinn í durum, ok köstuðust þeir á nökkurum orðum.	Bjarni went now to Sunnudal, and standing Thorstein in doorway, and exchanged they of some words.	Bjarni now went to Sunnudal and there was Thorstein standing in the doorway, and they exchanged some words.
Bjarni mælti:	Bjarni spoke:	Bjarni spoke:
"Þú skalt til einvigis ganga við mik í dag, Þórsteinn, á hól þenna, er hér er í tuni".	"You shall to single-combat go with me to day, Thorstein, on hill this, which here is in field".	"You shall go to single combat with me today Thorstein, on this hill which is here in the field.
"Allt er mér til þess vant",	"All is me to this difficulty",	"This is all to my difficulty",
segir Þórsteinn,	say Thorstein,	said Thorstein,
"at berjast við þik; enn ek skal þegar útan, er skip ganga, því at ek kenni drengskap þinn, at þú mant fá föður mínum forverk, er ek ferr frá".	"to fight with you; then I shall straightaway out-travel, with ship going, because that I know honour yours, that you would give father mine for-work, who I travel from".	"to fight with you, but I shall immediately travel out with the first ship going, because I know your honour, that you would give my father labour if I leave".

The Tale of Thorstein Staff-Struck (Old Norse)

Old Norse	Literal	English
"Eigi stoðar nú undan at mælast",	"Not avail now from-under that speak",	"You cannot speak to avail yourself out from under this",
segir Bjarni.	said Bjarni.	said Bjarni.
"Leyfa muntú mér þá at finna föður minn áðr",	"Allow shall-you for-me then that find father mine before",	"Will you allow me that I can find my father before",
segir Þórsteinn.	said Thorstein.	said Thorstein.
"At vísu",	"To-be certain",	"Certainly",
segir Bjarni.	said Bjarni.	said Bjarni.
Þórsteinn gekk inn, ok segir föður sínum, at Bjarni var þar kominn, ok bauð honum til einvígis.	Thorstein went inside, and told father his, that Bjarni was there coming, and invited him to single-combat.	Thorstein went inside and told his father that Bjarni was here and had invited him to single-combat.
Þórarinn karl svarar:	Thorarin old-man answered:	Thorarin, the old man, answered:
"Vera má hverr maðr þess vita, ef hann á við sér rikara mann, er siti samheraðs honum ok hafi þó gert honum nökkura ósœmd, at hann mun eigi mörgum skyrtum slita, ok kann ek því eigi at sýta þik, at mér þykkir þú margt hafa tilgert.	"Be may any man this know, if he to against himself more-powerful man, who situated same-district his and has though done him some dishonour, that he should not many shirts wear-out, and know I therefore not to mourn you, that to-me seens you many had to-do.	"Any man may know to expect this, if he has done some discredit against a more powerful man in his own district, that he will not wear out many more shirts, and I know therefore not to mourn you because it seems to me that you have done much.
Tak nú vápn þín ok ver þik sem skörugligast, því at þar mundi hafa verit minnar æfi, at eigi munda ek bograt hafa fyrir slikum sem Bjarni er, ok er Bjarni þo hinn mesti kappi.	Take now weapons yours and be you as noble, because that there would have been my life, that not would I stoop have before such as Bjarni is, and is Bjarni though the most warriors.	Now take your weapons and be noble, because in my life I would not have stooped before such a man as Bjarni is. Even though he is the best warrior.
Þykki mér ok betra at missa þín enn at eiga ragan son".	Consider I also better to miss you than to have coward a-son".	I consider it better to lose you than to have a coward for a son".

The Tale of Thorstein Staff-Struck (Old Norse)

Old Norse	Literal	English
# 6	# 6	# 6
Nú gengr Þórsteinn út, ok fara þeir síðan út á höllinn ok taka til at herjast með harðfengi, ok hjuggust mjök hlífar fyrir hvárumtveggja;	Now went Thorstein out, and went they afterwards out to the-hill and took to that fighting with toughness, and hewed much protection before each-other;	Now Thorstein went outside and then they went out to the hill and took to fighting with toughness and struck down much of each other's shields.
ok er þeir höfðu mjök lengi barizt, mælti Bjarni til Þórsteins;	and when they had much along carried, spoke Bjarni to Thorstein's;	And then when they had carried on for a long time, Bjarni spoke to Thorstein:
"Þyrstir mik nú, því at ek em óvanari erfiðinu enn þú".	"Thirsty me now, because that I am not-used-to difficulty as you".	"I am thirsty now because I am not used to such difficulty as you".
"Gakk þú þá til lækjarins",	"Go you then to stream",	"Then go to the stream",
segir Þórsteinn,	said Thorstein,	said Thorstein,
"ok drekk".	"and drink".	"and drink".
Bjarni gerði svá, ok lagði niðr sverðit hjá sér.	Bjarni did so, and had downed the-sword beside himself.	Bjarni did so and put his sword down beside himself.
Þórsteinn tók upp, leit á ok mælti.	Thorstein took up, looked at and spoke.	Thorstein took it up, looked at it, and spoke:
"Eigi mundir þú þetta sverð hafa í Böðvarsdal".	"Not would you this sword have at Bodvarsdale".	"You would not have had this sword at Bodvarsdale".
Bjarni svarar öngu.	Bjarni answered none.	Bjarni did not answer.
Ganga þeir nú enn uppá hólinn, ok berjast um stundarsakir.	Went they now then up hill, and fought about awhile's-sake.	Now they went up the hill and fought awhile,
Þykkir Bjarna maðrinn vígkœnn, ok þykkir fastlegra fyrir enn hann hugði.	Seemed Bjarni the-man battle-cunning, and seemed fixed before then he thought.	and Bjarni seemed convinced that Thorstein was a cunning fighter and the fight seemed more fixed than before.
"Margt hendir mik nú í dag",	"Many happens to-me now this day",	"Everything is happening to me today",
sagði Bjarni,	said Bjarni,	said Bjarni,
"lausir eru skópvengir mínir".	"loose are shoe-thongs mine".	"my shoe-thong is loose".

The Tale of Thorstein Staff-Struck (Old Norse)

Old Norse	Literal	English
"Bind þú þá",	"Tie you then",	"Then tie it",
segir Þórsteinn.	said Thorstein.	said Thorstein.
Nú lýtr Bjarni niðr, enn Þórsteinn gekk inn, ok hefir út skjöldu tvá ok sverð gott; gengr nú á hólinn til Bjarna, ok mælti við hann:	Now stooped Bjarni down, then Thorstein went inside, and had out shields two and sword one; went now in the-hill to Bjarni, and spoke with him:	Now Bjarni stooped down and then Thorstein went inside and brought out two shields and one sword and went to the hill to Bjarni and spoke with him:
"Hér er skjöldr ok sverð, er faðir minn sendi þér, ok mun þetta eigi slæfast meirr í höggunum enn þat er þú hefir áðr.	"Here is shield and sword, that father mine sent you, and should this not blunt more in the-blows than this which you had before.	"Here is a shield and sword that my father has sent you, and this should not be blunt with each blow like the sword you used before.
Nenni ek ok eigi at standa hlífarlauss undir höggum þínum; enn gjarnan vilda ek hætta þessum leik, því at ek er hræddr, at meira megi gæfa þín enn ógifta mín, ok er þó hverr frekr til fjörsins.	Care I also not to stand helpless under blows yours; then gladly will I conclude this sport, because that I am scared, that more may-be gift yours than un-gift mine, and that though each eager to life.	Also I do not care to stand helpless any longer under your blows and I would gladly conclude this sport because I am scared that your good luck shall be greater than my bad luck, and also each of us are eager to struggle to live,
Mun ek nú teljast undan um alla þraut framar meirr, ef ek mætta nökkuru um ráða".	Shall I now tell-you away-from about all struggle from-going more, if I may somewhat about decide".	and I would if I could decide it".
"Eigi man nú stoða at beiðast undan",	"Not should now stand to ask away-from",	"You should not try to ask your way out of it",
sagði Bjarni;	said Bjarni;	said Bjarni,
"berjast skal enn".	"fighting shall still".	"the fight must go on".
"Eigi mundak þá frekt höggva",	"Not would then eagerly strike",	"I wouldn't want to strike the first blow",
segir Þórsteinn.	said Thorstein.	said Thorstein.
Þá höggr Bjarni allan skjöldinn af Þórsteini, ok þá hjó Þórsteinn skjöldinn af Bjarna.	Then struck Bjarni all shield of Thorstein's, and then struck Thorstein shield of Bjarni's.	Then Bjarni struck and destroyed Thorstein's shield, and Thorstein struck and destroyed Bjarni's shield.
"Stórt er nú höggvið",	"Great is now the-blow",	"The striking is greater now",

The Tale of Thorstein Staff-Struck (Old Norse)

Old Norse	Literal	English
segir Bjarni.	said Bjarni.	said Bjarni.
Þórsteinn svarar:	Thorstein answered:	Thorstein answered:
"Eigi hjóstu smærra högg".	"Not have-you-hit a-smaller blow".	"Your strike was no smaller".
Bjarni mælti:	Bjarni spoke:	Bjarni spoke:
"Betr bítr þér nú hit sama sverðit, er þú hefir áðr haft í dag".	"Better bite you now then the-same sword, than you have before had in the-day".	"Now it bites better than the same weapon that you had before in the day".
Þórsteinn mælti:	Thorstein spoke:	Thorstein spoke:
"Spara munda ek mik við óhapp, ef ek mætta svá gera, ok berjumst ek hræddr við þik;	"Spare would I me with mishap, if I might so do, and fight I-am scared against you;	"I wish to spare myself from bad luck if I might do so, and I am scared to fight with you.
vilda ek enn allt á þínu valdi vera láta".	wish I then all to you will be had".	I wish for you to settle all of the matter".
Þá átti Bjarni at höggva, ok var nú hvárrtveggja hlífarlauss.	Then had Bjarni to strike, and was now each helpless.	Then it was Bjarni's turn to strike and now each man was helpless.
Bjarni mælti þá:	Bjarni spoke then:	Then Bjarni spoke:
"Þat mun illt kaup, at taka glœp við miklu happi.	"It should ill purchase, that takes the-wicked with much luck.	"It would ill afford to take much wickedness with luck.
Ætla ek mér fullgoldit fyrir þrjá húskarla mína þik einn, ef þú vilt mér trúr vera".	Suppose I myself fully-golded for three servants mine you alone, if you will to-me true be".	I would suppose myself fully paid for my three servants if you alone will serve me faithfully".
Þórsteinn mælti:	Thorstein said:	Thorstein said:
"Orðit hafa mér svá fœri á þér í dag, at ek mætta svíkja þik, ef ógæfa mín gengi ríkar enn gæfa þín; ok mun ek eigi svíkja þik",	"Words have me so brought in you in day, that I may betray you, if misfortune mine went stronger than gift yours; and should I not betray you",	"I have had many words with you today where I might have betrayed you if my misfortune was stronger than your luck, and so I will not betray you",
sagði Þórsteinn.	said Thorstein.	said Thorstein.

The Tale of Thorstein Staff-Struck (Old Norse)

Old Norse	Literal	English
"Sé ek at þú er afbragðs maðr", sagði Bjarni.	"See I that you are excellent man", said Bjarni.	"I see now that you are an excellent man", said Bjarni.
"Lofa muntú mér, at ek ganga inn til föður þíns",	"Promise shall-you me, that I go inside to father yours",	"You will promise me that I go inside to your father",
segir hann,	said he,	he said,
"ok segi honum slíkt er ek vil".	"and tell him such who I wish".	"and tell him about this as I wish".
"Gakk sem þú vilt fyrir mínum sóknum",	"Go as you wish for my sake",	"Go as you wish, for my sake",
sagði Þórsteinn	said Thorstein	said Thorstein,
"ok far þó varlega".	"and go though warily".	"and go carefully".

7 | # 7 | # 7

Old Norse	Literal	English
Þá gekk Bjarni inn, ok at lokhvílu þefri, er Þórarinn karl lá í.	Then went Bjarni in, and to bed-closet there, where Thorarin old-man lay in.	Then Bjarni went in to the bed closet where Thorarin the old man was laying.
Þórarinn spurði, hverr þar fœri? Bjarni sagði til sín.	Thorarin asked, who there went? Bjarni told to him.	Thorarin then asked who went there and Bjarni told him.
"Hvat segir þú tíðinda, Bjarni minn?"	"What say you news, Bjarni mine?"	"What news do you speak about, my Bjarni?",
segir Þórarinn.	say Thorarin.	said Thorarin.
"Víg Þórsteins sonar þíns",	"Killing Thorstein son yours",	"The killing of your son",
segir Bjarni.	said Bjarni.	said Bjarni.
"Varðist hann nökkut?"	"Defended he any-at-all?"	"Did he defend himself at all?",
segir Þórarinn.	say Thorarin.	said Thorarin.
"Engan mann ætla ek snarligra verit hafa í vápnaskiftum enn Þórstein son þinn", segir Bjarni.	"None man suppose I speedily have had in weapons-exchange than Thorstein a-son yours", said Bjarni.	"I do not think I have been in such a speedy exchange of weapons as with your son Thorstein".
"Eigi er kynlegt at því",	"Not is wonder that therefore",	"It is no wonder therefore",

The Tale of Thorstein Staff-Struck (Old Norse)

Old Norse	Literal	English
segir karl,	said the-old-man,	said the old man,
"at þungt veitti við þik í Böðvarsdal, er þú bart nú af syni mínum".	"that difficulty granted with you at Bodvarsdale, that you overcome now of son mine".	"that you granted such difficulty to those at Bodvarsdale, that you have now overcome my son".
Þá mælti Bjarni:	Then spoke Bjarni:	Then Bjarni spoke:
"Ek vil bjóða þér til Hofs, ok skaltú sitja þar í öðru öndvegi meðan þá liflr, ok mun ek vera þér í sonar stað".	"I wish to-invite you to Hof, and shall-you settle there in another foremost-seat as-long-as then live, and should I be to-you in son's place".	"I wish to invite you to Hof, and you shall settle there in one of the foremost seats as long as you live, and I shall be in your son's place".
"Svá er mér farit",	"So is to-me going",	"So it goes to me",
segir karl,	said the-old-man,	said the old man,
"sem þeim, er eigi eigu undir sér, ok verðr heitum heimskr maðr feginn.	"which those, who not only submit to-you, and worth called stupid man joyful.	"that those who do not alone accept you and your promise joyfully are stupid.
Enn svá eru heit yðor höfðingja, þá er þér vilit fróa mann eftir slíka atburði, at þat er mánaðar-frá; enn eftir þat eru vér virðir sem aðrir framfœrslumenn, ok fyrnast við þat seint várir harmar.	But so are promises of-you chieftains, then that you wish console people after such events, that it is a-month-from; then after that they-are we valued as-if other paupers, and age with it weak our harm.	But so are the promises of you chieftains whom you wish to console after such events, that a month from then they are valued as paupers and their harm does not weaken with age.
Enn sá maðr þriflst aldregi, er ekki tekr	Then so the-man thrives never, who not takes	Still, the man who takes a pledge with such a man as you may well be deemed to be content with his lot.
handsöl afþér, ok gakk þú nú hingat til mín í rekkjugólfit, ok verðr þú nær at ganga, því at karl skelfr nú allr á fótum fyrir elli sakir ok vanheilsu, enn eigi trútt, at mér hafi eigi í skap runnit sonar-dauðinn".	pledge of-you, and come you now here to me in bed-closet, and become you near to going, because that old-man shaking now all on feet for age sake and failing-health, but none truth, to to-me has not in mood slipped son-death".	So I should also take this pledge with you, and now come here to me in the bed closet and come nearer because I am an old man shaking on his feet for the sake of age and ill health, but one truth alone has caused my mood to slip, the death of my son".
Bjarni gekk nú í rekkjugólfit í hendr Þórarins karls.	Bjarni went now into bed-closet in hand Thorarin the-old-man.	Bjarni now went into the bed closet and took Thorarin the old man's hand.

The Tale of Thorstein Staff-Struck (Old Norse)

Old Norse	Literal	English
Hann fann, at hann þuklaði á saxi, ok vildi þá leggja til Bjarna.	He found, that he felt a short-sword, and willed then to-lay to Bjarni.	He then found that he felt a short sword that he wished to lay at Bjarni.
Hann kipti hendinni ok mælti:	He dragged his-hand and spoke:	He drew his hand and spoke:
"Allra fretkarla armastr.	"All contemptible-man miserable.	"You are an all contemptible and miserable man",
Men nú at makligleikum fara með okkr.	But now it serves-you-right going between us.	"How it will serve you right what happens between us.
Þórsteinn sonr þinn lifir, ok skal hann fara heim með mér til Hofs, enn þér skal fá þræla til forverka, ok skal þér engis vant meðan þú lifir".	Thorstein son yours alive, and shall he travel home with me to Hof, then you shall get thralls to working, and shall you nothing want as-long-as you live".	Thorstein your son is alive and he shall travel home with me to Hof, and you shall get servants to work for you and you shall want for nothing as long as you live".
Þórsteinn fór nú heim með Bjarna til Hofs, ok fylgdi honum allt til dauða-dags, ok þótti nær engis manns maki vera at drengskap ok hreysti.	Thorstein travelled now home with Bjarni to Hof, and followed him all until death-day, and thought near only man matched had-been that honour and valour.	Now Thorstein travelled home with Bjarni to Hof and followed him in everything until the day he died, and he was thought the only man near to matching him in honour and valour.

8

Bjarni helt virðingu sinni, ok var hann því vinsælli ok betr stilltr sem hann var ellri, ok var allra manna þrautbeztr ok gerðist trú-maðr mikill hinn siðara hlut ævi sinnar.	Bjarni held worthiness his, and was he therefore popular and better orderly as he was older, and were all men persistent and became true-man great the last part life his.	Bjarni held his standing well and became more popular and more self-controlled as he got older, and he was of all men the most persistent, and he became a great man of true faith for the last part of his life.
Bjarni fór útan ok gekk suðr, ok andaðist í þeiri ferð.	Bjarni travelled out and went south, and died on their journey.	Bjarni travelled abroad and went south and died on that journey.
Hann hvílir í borg þeiri, er Valería heitir, ok er þat mikil borg skamt hingat frá Rúmaborg.	He rested in Borg there, was Sutri named, and was that great Borg short there from Rome-city.	He rested at a city that was named Sutri, and that was a great city, a short distance from the city of Rome.

The Tale of Thorstein Staff-Struck (Old Norse)

Old Norse	Literal	English
Hans son var Skegg-Broddi, er víða kemr við sögur, ok var hinn mesti afbragðsmaðr um sína daga.	His a-son was Skegg-Broddi, who widely came in the-sagas, and was the most outstanding-man about his day.	His son was Beard-Broddi who appears widely in the sagas, and he was the most outstanding man of his day.
Dóttir Bjarna hét Halla, ok Guðríðr, er Kolbeinn lögsögumaðr átti.	Daughter Bjarni's named Halla, and Gudrid, who Kolbein lawspeaker married.	Bjarni had a daughter named Halla, the mother of Gudrid, who married Kolbein the lawspeaker.
Ingveldr var ok dóttir Bjarna, er Þórsteinn Siðu-Hallsson átti, ok var þeira son Magnus, faðir Einars, föður Magnúsar biskups.	Yngvild was also daughter Bjarni's, was Thorstein Sidu-Hallson married, and was their son Magnus, father-of Einar, father-of Magnus the-bishop.	Bjarni had another daughter named Yngvild who married Thorstein Sidu-Hallson, their son was Magnus, the father of Einar, the father of Magnus the bishop.
Ögmundr var ok sonr Þórsteins ok Ingveldra;	Amundi was also son Thorstein's and Yngvild's;	Thorstein and Yngvild also had a son named Amundi.
hann átti Sigríði dóttur Þórgríms blinda,	he married Sigrid daughter Thorgrim's the-blind,	He married Sigrid, the daughter of Thorgrim the blind.
Þeira dóttir (var) Hallfríðr móðir (Ámunda), föður Guðmundar, föður Magnúss góða ok Þóru, móður Gissurar jarls, ok annarrar Þórn, móður Orms Svínfellings.	Their daughter (was) Hallfrid mother-of (Amundi's), father Gudmund's, father-of Magnus the-chieftain and Thora, mother-of Gissurar the-earl, and of-the-other Thora, mother-of Orm Svinafellings.	Amundi also had a daughter named Hallfrid, the mother of Amundi, the father of Gudmund, the father of the chieftain Magnus, and of Thora who married Thorvald Gizurarson, and the other Thora who was the mother of Orm of Svinafell.
Guðrún var ok dóttir Ögmundar, móðir Þórdísar, móður Helgu, móður Guðnýjar, móður Sturlusona: Þórðar, Sighvats og Snorra.	Gudrun was and daughter Ogmund, mother-of Thordis, mother-of Helga, mother-of Gudny, mother-of The-Sturlusons: Thord, Sighvat and Snorri.	Amundi had another daughter called Gudrun, the mother of Thordis, the mother of Helga, the mother of Gudny Bodvar's daughter, the mother of the Sturlusons, Thord, Sighvat, and Snorri.
Rannveig var ok dóttir Ögmundar, móðir Steins, föður Guðrúnar, móður Árnfríðar, er Digr-Helgi átti.	Rannveig was and daughter-of Ogmund, mother-of Stein, father Gudrun, mother-of , who had.	Amundi also had a daughter named Rannveig, the mother of Stein, the father of Gudrun, the mother of Arnfrid, who was married to Stout-Helgi.

The Tale of Thorstein Staff-Struck (Old Norse)

Old Norse	Literal	English
Þórkatla var ok dóttir Ögmundar, móðir Arnbjargar, móður Jóns prests ok Þórgeirs ok Þuriðar,	Thorkatla was and daughter-of Ogmund, mother-of Arnbjorg, mother-of Jon the-priest and Thorgeir and Thorid,	Thorkatla was also a daughter of Amundi, the mother of Arnbjorg, the mother of Fin the priest, and Thorgeir and Thurid.
ok er margt störmenna frá þeim komit.	and are many prestigious-people from them coming.	And there were many prestigious people descended from them.
Ok lýkr hér sögu-þætti Þórsteins stangarhöggs.	And ends here the-saga-tale Thorstein Staff-Struck.	And there ends the saga of Thorstein Staff-Struck.

Word List (Old Norse to English)

Old Norse	English

A, a

aðrir	other
af	of, of, off
afbragðs	excellent
afbragðsmaðr	outstanding-man
aftan	evening
afþér	of-you
aldregi	never
alla	all
allan	all
allmargt	all-many
allr	all
allra	all
allt	all, all
alvöru	seriously
andaðist	died
annarr	another, one
annarra	other
annarrar	of-the-other
annarri	another
annars	another's
armastr	miserable
Arnbjargar	Arnbjorg (name)
at	at, it, it, that, to, than, that, to, to-be
atburð	accident
atburði	events
augat	eye

Á, á

á	a, about, at, in, of, on, to
áðr	before
Ámunda	Amundi's (name)
árnfríðar	0
átt	had
átti	had, married
áttu	had

Æ, æ

æfi	life
ætla	suppose
ætlar	suppose
ætluðu	intended
ætlum	suppose
ævi	life

B, b

bað	asked
báða	both
bæði	both
bak	back
banahögg	death-blow
bar	carried
barizt	carried
bart	overcome
batt	bound
bauð	invited
beiðast	ask
bekk	bench
berjast	fight, fighting, fought
berjumst	fight
best	the-horse
betr	better
betra	better
biða	abide
biðr	asked
bind	tie
bindr	tied
biskups	the-bishop
bítast	bite
bítr	bite
Bjarna	Bjarni (name), Bjarni's (name)
Bjarni	Bjarni (name)
bjó	lived
bjóða	to-invite
björg	help

Word List (Old Norse to English)

Old Norse	English
blinda	the-blind
Böðvarsdal	Bodvarsdale (name)
bœta	compensation
bœtrnur	compensation
bograt	stoop
bolinn	torso
borð	the-table
borða	the-tables
borði	the-table
Borg	Borg (place)
bræðr	brothers
bregð	move
brugðust	broke
brúnina	eyebrow
búi	estate
búit	prepared
bústú	settle
býr	prepared

D, d

Old Norse	English
dældarmaðr	gentle-man
dag	day, the-day
daga	day
dagmálum	mid-morning
dauða-dags	death-day
digr-helgi	0
dilka-höfuð	sheep-heads
dœmi	judging
dóttir	daughter, daughter-of
dóttur	daughter
draga	drag
drekk	drink
drengskap	honour
drepit	killed
dugi	spirit
durum	doorway

E, e

Old Norse	English
eðr	or
ef	if
eftir	after
eggja	encouraging
eiga	have
eigi	none, not, not-be
eigu	only
eina	one
Einars	Einar (name)
einn	alone, one
einum	one
einvigis	single-combat
einvígis	single-combat
eitt	one-thing
ek	I, I-am
ekki	not
eldhúsveggnum	fire-house-wall
elli	age
ellri	older
em	am
en	and
engan	none
engi	none, no-one, nothing
engir	none
engis	nothing, only
enn	and, as, but, still, than, then, when
er	am, are, as, at, but, is, is-it, than, that, was, what, when, where, which, who, who-are, with
erfiðinu	difficulty
erindislaust	errand-lost
ert	are
ertú	are-you
eru	are, are-you, they-are, were
erum	are

É, é

Old Norse	English
énn	but

F, f

Old Norse	English
fá	few, get, give
faðir	father, father-of
fann	found

Word List (Old Norse to English)

Old Norse	English
far	go, Travel
fara	going, to-go, to-travel, travel, travelled, went
farinn	gone
farit	going, gone
fastlegra	fixed
feðgar	father-and-son
feginn	joyful
fekk	got
félitill	fee-little
fell	fell
ferð	journey
ferr	travel, travelled
finna	find
finnim	finding
fjár	fee
fjölmenni	followers
fjölmennr	followers
fjörsins	life
flekk	stain
fóður	father
föður	father, father-of
fœra	bring, travelled
fœri	brought, went
fœrir	brought
fór	travelled, went
för	for
forlagðir	mislaid
forverk	for-work
forverka	working
fótum	feet
frá	from
frændi	kinsmen
frændum	kinsmen
framar	from-going
framfœrslumenn	paupers
frekr	eager
frekt	eagerly
fretkarla	contemptible-man
fróa	console
frýju-orð	taunting
fullgoldit	fully-golded
fylgdi	followed
fyrir	before, for
fyrnast	age

G, g

Old Norse	English
gæfa	gift
gætti	guarded
gakk	come, go
gamall	old
ganga	go, going, went
garð	fences
garðinu	meadow
gegnum	through
gekk	went
geldinga-höfuð	ram-heads
gengi	went
gengr	went
gengu	went
gera	do
gerði	did
gerðist	became
gerðú	do-you
gerir	make
gert	done
gissurar	Gissurar
gjarnan	gladly
glœp	the-wicked
góða	the-chieftain
gott	one
gráta	weeping
Guðmundar	Gudmund's (name)
Guðnýjar	Gudny (name)
Guðríðr	Gudrid (name)
Guðrún	Gudrun (name)
Guðrúnar	Gudrun (name)

H, h

Old Norse	English
hætta	conclude, concluded, risk
hafa	had, have
hafði	had
hafi	had, has, have
haft	had
hála	neck
haldkvæmara	hold-fulfil
halds	hold

Word List (Old Norse to English)

Old Norse	English
Halla	Halla (name)
Hallfríðr	Hallfrid (name)
hana	her
handsöl	pledge
hann	he, him
hans	him, his
happi	luck
harðfengi	toughness
harmar	harm
haustit	autumn
höggunum	the-blows
hefi	have
hefir	had, has, have
hefna	revenge
heill	healthy
heim	home
heima	home
heiman	home
heimskr	stupid
heimta	claim
heit	promises
heitir	named
heitum	called
heldr	rather
Helgu	Helga (name)
heljarmannsins	cursed-man-this
helt	held
helzt	rather
hendi	arms
hendinni	his-hand
hendir	happens
hendr	hand, hands
hér	here
heraðinu	the-district
herjast	fighting
hesta	horses
hesta-ats	horse-fight
hestana	horses
hestarnir	the-horses
hestastafnum	horse-staffs
hestasvein	horse-boy
hestaþingi	horse-fight
hesta-þinginu	horse-fight
hesthúsinn	horse-house
hesti	horse
hestr	horse
hestum	horses
hestunum	horses
hét	named, was-named
hey	hay
heyrðu	heard
hiífar	protection
hingat	here, there
hinir	they
hinn	the
hit	then
hitta	met
hitti	met
hittir	found
hjá	beside
hjó	struck
hjóstu	have-you-hit
hjuggust	hewed
hleypr	ran
hlífarlauss	helpless
hljóp	ran
hlut	part
hlýða	listen
hlýddi	followed
höfði	head
höfðingja	chieftains
höfðu	had
Hofi	Hof (place)
hofs	Hof, Hof (place)
höfuð	head
höfuðbeinum	head-bone
högg	a-strike, been-struck, blow, striking
höggr	struck
höggum	blows
höggva	strike
höggvið	the-blow
hól	hill
hólinn	hill
hölinn	the-hill
höllinn	the-hill
hon	her, it, she
honum	he, him, his
hræddr	scared
hrósit	praise
hreysti	valour

Word List (Old Norse to English)

Old Norse	English
hrossa	horses, the-horses
hrossahúsi	horse-house
hrossahússins	horse-house
hrossamaðr	horse-man
hrossin	horses
hug	thoughts
hugða	thought
hugði	thought
hundr	a-dog
húskarl	servant
húskarla	servants
húskarlar	servants
húss	house
hváftana	mouths
hvar	where
hvarf	disappeared
hvárn	each
hvárrtveggja	each
hvárt	whether
hvárumtveggja	each-other
hvat	what
hvatti	sharpened
hvenær	when
hvernig	how
hverr	any, each, who, why
hversu	how-many
hvert	what, which
hvi	Why
hvílir	rested

I, i

illt	ill
Ingveldr	Yngvild (name)
Ingveldra	Yngvild's (name)
inn	in, inside

Í, í

í	at, in, into, on, this, to

J, j

Old Norse	English
jafnhátt	equally
jarða	buried
jarðaðr	earthed
jarls	the-earl
Jól	Yule (name)
Jóns	Jon (name)

K, k

kalla	call
kallaðr	called
kals	taunted
kann	know
kappi	warriors
karl	old-man, the-old-man
karls	the-old-man
kaup	purchase
kemr	came, comes
kenna	be-known
kenni	know
kipti	dragged
kné	knees
Kolbeinn	Kolbein (name)
kölluðu	called
kom	came
koma	came
kominn	came, come, coming
komit	coming
komnir	coming
kona	the-woman
konan	the-woman
konu	woman
konum	women
konur	women
köstuðust	exchanged
kvað	said
kváðust	said
kvenna	women
kynlegt	surprised, wonder
kyrt	peace, still

L, l

lá	lay

Word List (Old Norse to English)

Old Norse	English	*Old Norse*	English
lægi	laying	mælti	said, spoke
lætr	behaved, had, has	mæltu	spoke-of
lagði	had	mætta	may, might
lágði	laid	Magnus	Magnus (name)
lagðist	laid	Magnúsar	Magnus (name)
lambahöfuðin	lambs-heads	Magnúss	Magnus (name)
láta	had	maki	matched
lausir	loose	makligleikum	serves-you-right
laust	struck	málit	a-case
leggja	to-lay	man	shall, should
leið	pass	mánaðar-frá	a-month-from
leik	sport	mann	man, people
leit	looked	manna	men, people's
leita	look-for, looking-for	manns	man, man's
lengi	along	mant	shall, would
lengr	along	mantú	should
lét	had	marga	many
letja	discourage	margir	many
leyfa	allow	margt	many
leyna	keep-secret	með	between, with
líðr	passed	meðan	as-long-as
lifir	alive, live	megi	may-be
liflr	live	meira	more
liklegastir	likeliest	meirr	more
litlu	little	men	but
lítt	little	menn	men, people
lœkjarins	stream	mér	for-me, I, me, met, myself, to-me
lofa	promise		
lögsögumaðr	lawspeaker	mesti	most
lokhvílu	bed-closet	meta	meet
lostinn	struck	mik	me, meet, to-me
lýkr	ends	mikil	great
lýstr	struck	mikill	great
lýtr	stooped	mikit	much
		miklar	much
		miklir	much

M, m

		miklu	much
		min	me
má	may	mín	mine
maðr	a-man, man, the-man	mína	mine
maðrinn	the-man	mínir	mine
mæl	say	minn	mine
mæla	speak	minnar	my
mælast	speak	minni	mine
mælir	speak	mínum	mine, my
mælt	speaking, spoken	mislagðar	misplaced

Word List (Old Norse to English)

Old Norse	English
missa	miss
mjök	much
móðir	mother-of
móður	mother-of
mörgum	many
morgun	morning
morguninn	morning
móti	towards
mun	shall, should
munda	would
mundak	would
mundi	could, thought, would
mundir	would
mundu	would
mundum	would
muni	would
muntú	shall-you

N, n

Old Norse	English
nær	near
naut	a-bull, bull
né	nor
nefndr	named
nenni	bothers, care
nenta	wanted
niðr	down, downed
nökkura	some
nökkuru	somewhat
nökkurum	some
nökkut	any-at-all
nóttina	the-night
nú	now

O, o

Old Norse	English
of	of
ofan	across, down, over
ofmælt	said-too-much
oft	often
oftar	often
og	and
ok	also, and
okkr	us
oklíklegt	and-likely
orð	words
orða	words
orðit	worded, words
orðum	words
Orms	Orm (name)
oss	us, we

Ó, ó

Old Norse	English
ógæfa	misfortune
ógifta	un-gift
óhapp	mishap
óhefnt	without-revenge
ójafnaðar	un-equal-man
ómegð	without
ómjúkir	unremarkable
ór	from
ósœmd	dishonour
óvanari	not-used-to

Ö, ö

Old Norse	English
öðru	another
öðrum	other, the-other
öflugr	powerful
Ögmundar	Ogmund (name)
Ögmundr	Amundi (name)
öllu	all
öndvegi	foremost-seat
öngu	none
ör	out-of
öttu	matched
öxina	axe

Œ, œ

Old Norse	English
œptu	called-out
œsku	youth

P, p

Word List (Old Norse to English)

Old Norse	English
prests	the-priest

R, r

Old Norse	English
ráða	decide
ragan	coward, cowardly
rann	ran
Rannveig	Rannveig (name)
reið	ride
reiðhesta	riding-horses
reis	rose
reist	carved
rekkjugðlfit	bed-closet
rekkjugólfit	bed-closet
ríkar	stronger
rikara	more-powerful
riks	noble
rísa	rose
rœða	discussing
Rúmaborg	Rome-city (place)
runnit	slipped

S, s

Old Norse	English
sá	saw, so
sæng	bed
sæti	sat
sagði	said, said, told
sagt	told
sakir	sake
saklausa	without-cause
sama	the-same
saman	together
samheraðs	same-district
sárunum	injury
sat	sat
satt	TRUE
sátu	sat
sax	short-sword
saxi	short-sword
saxinu	short-sword
sé	is, see
seg	tell
segi	say, tell
segir	said, say, told
segja	tell, told
seint	weak
sekan	guilty
seldu	sold
sem	as, as-if, which
sendi	sent
sér	himself, themselves, to-you
síðan	afterwards, then
síðar	afterwards
siðara	last
Siðu-Hallsson	Sidu-Hallson (name)
Sighvats	Sighvat (name)
Sigríði	Sigrid (name)
sín	him, his
sína	his, theirs
sinn	his
sinnar	his
sinni	his
síns	hers, his
sínu	his
sínum	his, theirs
siti	situated
sitja	settle
sitt	yours
sjálfbjarga	self-supported
sjálfr	himself, myself
sjðnlausum	sight-less
sjónlitill	seeing-little
skal	shall
skalt	shall
skaltú	shall, shall-you
skamt	short
skap	mood
skapi	mind
Skegg-Broddi	Skegg-Broddi (name)
skelfr	shaking
skifta	exchange
skilit	divided
skip	ship
skjöldinn	shield
skjöldr	shield
skjöldu	shields
skógarmaðr	outlaw
skógarmaðrinn	outlawed

Word List (Old Norse to English)

Old Norse	English
skoltinn	jaw
skörugligast	noble
skóþvengir	shoe-thongs
skyldi	should, should-be
skyldu	should
skyrtublaði	shirt-sheet
skyrtum	shirts
slæfast	blunt
slika	such
slíka	such
slíkt	such
slikum	such
slita	wear-out
smærra	a-smaller
snarligra	speedily
snemma	early
Snorra	Snorri (name)
sofa	slept
sögur	the-sagas
sögu-þætti	the-saga-tale
sóknum	sake
son	a-son, son
sonar	son, son's
sonar-dauðinn	son-death
sonr	son
spara	spare
spurði	asked
spyrr	asked
stað	place
stakk	pushed
standa	stand
Stangarhögg	Staff-Struck (name)
Stangarhöggs	Staff-Struck (name)
stangat	gored
stðrmenna	prestigious-people
sté	stepped
Steins	Stein (name)
stendr	standing
stilltr	orderly
stiltr	composed
stóð	stood
stoða	stand
stoðar	avail, support
stóðhross	stud-horses
stórt	great
stundarsakir	awhile's-sake
stundu	time
Sturlusona	the-Sturlusons (name)
sú	that
suðr	south
sumar	summer
Sunnudal	Sunnudal (place)
svá	so
svarar	answered
svefns	sleep
sverð	sword
sverðit	sword, the-sword
svíða	singe
sviðelda	bonfires
sviðit	singe
svíkja	betray
svima	dizziness
Svínfellings	Svinafellings (name)
svivirðing	worthy
svöruðu	answered
syni	son
sýnist	seems
sýta	mourn

T, t

Old Norse	English
tak	take
taka	take, takes, took
talat	talking, told
tali	talking
tals	talk
taumana	reins
tekr	takes, took
teljast	tell-you
tiðast	news
tíðast	news
tíðinda	news
til	there, to, towards, until
tíl	to
tilgert	to-do
tilræði	assault
títt	reported
togat	pulled

Word List (Old Norse to English)

Old Norse	English
tók	took
tókum	taking
troll	trolls
trú-maðr	true-man
trúr	TRUE
trútt	truth
tungu	tongue
tungunni	tongue
tuni	field
tvá	two

Þ, þ

Old Norse	English
þá	then
það	that
þaðan	from
þær	there
þagat	silence
þar	there
þarf	needs
þat	it, it, that, this
þau	then, they
Þórarinn	Thorarin (name)
Þórsteinn	Thorstein (name)
þefri	there
þegar	straightaway
þeim	their, them, those
þeir	they
þeira	their, they, those
þeiri	their, there
þenna	this
þér	to-you, you, you-two
þess	this
þessarra	this
þessu	this
þessum	this
þetta	that, this
þik	you
þín	you, yours
þína	yours
þingmönnum	assembly-men
þings	the-assembly
þinn	yours
þíns	yours
þínu	you
þínum	you, yours
þit	this
þo	though
þó	though
þoli	tolerate
Þórarinn	Thorarin (name)
Þórarins	Thorarin (name)
Þórð	Thord (name)
Þórðar	Thord (name), Thord's (name)
Þórdísar	Thordis (name)
Þórðr	Thord (name)
Þórgeirs	Thorgeir (name)
Þórgríms	Thorgrim's (name)
Þórhall	Thorhall (name)
Þórhallr	Thorhall (name)
Þórkatla	Thorkatla (name)
Þórn	Thora (name)
Þórstein	Thorstein (name)
Þórsteini	Thorstein (name), Thorstein's (name)
Þórsteinn	Thorstein (name)
Þórsteins	Thorstein (name), Thorstein's (name)
Þóru	Thora (name)
Þórvald	Thorvald (name)
Þórvaldr	Thorvald (name)
þótt	though
þótti	thought
þræla	thralls
þraut	struggle
þrautbeztr	persistent
þrek	strength
þriflst	thrives
þriggja	three
þrjá	three
þú	you
þuklaði	felt
þungt	difficulty
þurfa	need
Þuriðar	Thorid (name)
því	accordingly, because, since, therefore, which
þykki	consider, seems, think

Word List (Old Norse to English)

Old Norse	English
þykkir	seem, seemed, seeming, seems, seens, think
þykkja	to-think
þykkjast	consider, thought
þyrstir	thirsty

U, u

Old Norse	English
um	about
undan	away, away-from, from-under
undir	submit, under, up-to
ungum	young
unz	until
upp	got-up, up
uppá	up
uppaustrarmenn	gossipers

Ú, ú

Old Norse	English
út	out, outside
útan	out, out-travel
úti	out, outside

V, v

Old Norse	English
váðaverk	accident, an-accident
vægt	mercy
vænt	expect
væri	was, would
vaknar	awoke
vakti	awoke
valdi	will
Valería	Sutri (place)
vanheilsu	failing-health
vann	worked
vant	difficulty, want
vápn	weapon, weapons
vápna	weapons
vápnaskiftum	weapons-exchange
var	was, were
vara	would-be

Old Norse	English
varð	was
varði	expected
varðist	defended
varðveitti	looked-after
várir	our
varlega	warily
varnaði	warn
vartú	were-you
váru	were
veginn	killed
vegit	killed
veit	know
veita	to-give
veitti	granted
vekja	wake
vel	well
ver	be
vér	we, we-are
vera	be, had-been
verða	be, became, become, comes
verðr	become, worth
verit	been, have
verk	work
verks	work
verr	worse, worst
verra	worse
vetrinn	winter
við	against, in, with
víða	widely
vig	killing
Víga-Bjarna	Killer-Bjarni (name)
vigit	the-killing
vígkœnn	battle-cunning
víkingr	viking
vil	wish
vilda	will, wish
vildi	willed, would
vilit	wish
vilja	will, wish
vill	will
vilt	will, wish
vinna	win
vinsælli	popular
virðingu	honour, worthiness
virðir	valued

Word List (Old Norse to English)

Old Norse   English

visar	saw
vísar	refer
vist	hospitality, provisions
víst	certain, knew
vísu	certain
vit	with
vita	know, known
víti	penalty
vits	wits
vitum	know

Y, y

yðr	you
yður	of-you
yfir	over

Word List *(English to Old Norse)*

English	Old Norse
a	á
abide	biða
about	á, um
a-bull	naut
a-case	málit
accident	atburð, váðaverk
accordingly	því
across	ofan
a-dog	hundr
after	eftir
afterwards	síðan, síðar
against	við
age	elli, fyrnast
alive	lifir
all	alla, allan, allr, allra, allt, allt, öllu
all-many	allmargt
allow	leyfa
alone	einn
along	lengi, lengr
also	ok
am	em, er
a-man	maðr
a-month-from	mánaðar-frá
Amundi (name)	Ögmundr
Amundi's (name)	Ámunda
an-accident	váðaverk
and	en, enn, og, ok
and-likely	oklíklegt
another	annarr, annarri, öðru
another's	annars
answered	svarar, svöruðu
any	hverr
any-at-all	nökkut
are	er, ert, eru, erum
are-you	ertú, eru
arms	hendi
Arnbjorg (name)	Arnbjargar
as	enn, er, sem
as-if	sem
ask	beiðast
asked	bað, biðr, spurði, spyrr
as-long-as	meðan
a-smaller	smærra
a-son	son
assault	tilræði
assembly-men	þingmönnum
a-strike	högg
at	á, at, er, í
autumn	haustit
avail	stoðar
away	undan
away-from	undan
awhile's-sake	stundarsakir
awoke	vaknar, vakti
axe	öxina

B, b

English	Old Norse
back	bak
battle-cunning	vígkœnn
be	ver, vera, verða
became	gerðist, verða
because	því
become	verða, verðr
bed	sæng
bed-closet	lokhvílu, rekkjugðlfit, rekkjugólfit
been	verit
been-struck	högg
before	áðr, fyrir
behaved	lætr
be-known	kenna
bench	bekk
beside	hjá
betray	svíkja
better	betr, betra
between	með
bite	bítast, bítr
Bjarni (name)	Bjarna, Bjarni
Bjarni's (name)	Bjarna
blow	högg

Word List (English to Old Norse)

English	Old Norse
blows	höggum
blunt	slæfast
Bodvarsdale (name)	Böðvarsdal
bonfires	sviðelda
Borg (place)	Borg
both	báða, bæði
bothers	nenni
bound	batt
bring	fœra
broke	brugðust
brothers	bræðr
brought	fœri, fœrir
bull	naut
buried	jarða
but	enn, énn, er, men

C, c

English	Old Norse
call	kalla
called	heitum, kallaðr, kölluðu
called-out	œptu
came	kemr, kom, koma, kominn
care	nenni
carried	bar, barizt
carved	reist
certain	víst, vísu
chieftains	höfðingja
claim	heimta
come	gakk, kominn
comes	kemr, verða
coming	kominn, komit, komnir
compensation	bœta, bœtrnur
composed	stiltr
conclude	hætta
concluded	hætta
consider	þykki, þykkjast
console	fróa
contemptible-man	fretkarla
could	mundi
coward	ragan
cowardly	ragan
cursed-man-this	heljarmannsins

D, d

English	Old Norse
daughter	dóttir, dóttur
daughter-of	dóttir
day	dag, daga
death-blow	banahögg
death-day	dauða-dags
decide	ráða
defended	varðist
did	gerði
died	andaðist
difficulty	erfiðinu, þungt, vant
disappeared	hvarf
discourage	letja
discussing	rœða
dishonour	ósœmd
divided	skilit
dizziness	svima
do	gera
done	gert
doorway	durum
down	niðr, ofan
downed	niðr
do-you	gerðú
drag	draga
dragged	kipti
drink	drekk

E, e

English	Old Norse
each	hvárn, hvárrtveggja, hverr
each-other	hvárumtveggja
eager	frekr
eagerly	frekt
early	snemma
earthed	jarðaðr
Einar (name)	Einars
encouraging	eggja
ends	lýkr
equally	jafnhátt
errand-lost	erindislaust
estate	búi
evening	aftan

Word List (English to Old Norse)

English	Old Norse
events	atburði
excellent	afbragðs
exchange	skifta
exchanged	köstuðust
expect	vænt
expected	varði
eye	augat
eyebrow	brúnina

F, f

English	Old Norse
failing-health	vanheilsu
father	faðir, fóður, föður
father-and-son	feðgar
father-of	faðir, föður
fee	fjár
fee-little	félitill
feet	fótum
fell	fell
felt	þuklaði
fences	garð
few	fá
field	tuni
fight	berjast, berjumst
fighting	berjast, herjast
find	finna
finding	finnim
fire-house-wall	eldhúsveggnum
fixed	fastlegra
followed	fylgdi, hlýddi
followers	fjölmenni, fjölmennr
for	för, fyrir
foremost-seat	öndvegi
for-me	mér
for-work	forverk
fought	berjast
found	fann, hittir
from	frá, ór, þaðan
from-going	framar
from-under	undan
fully-golded	fullgoldit

G, g

English	Old Norse
gentle-man	dældarmaðr
get	fá
gift	gæfa
Gissurar	gissurar
give	fá
gladly	gjarnan
go	far, gakk, ganga
going	fara, farit, ganga
gone	farinn, farit
gored	stangat
gossipers	uppaustrarmenn
got	fekk
got-up	upp
granted	veitti
great	mikil, mikill, stórt
guarded	gætti
Gudmund's (name)	Guðmundar
Gudny (name)	Guðnýjar
Gudrid (name)	Guðríðr
Gudrun (name)	Guðrún, Guðrúnar
guilty	sekan

H, h

English	Old Norse
had	átt, átti, áttu, hafa, hafði, hafi, haft, hefir, höfðu, lætr, lagði, láta, lét
had-been	vera
Halla (name)	Halla
Hallfrid (name)	Hallfríðr
hand	hendr
hands	hendr
happens	hendir
harm	harmar
has	hafi, hefir, lætr
have	eiga, hafa, hafi, hefi, hefir, verit
have-you-hit	hjóstu
hay	hey
he	hann, honum
head	höfði, höfuð
head-bone	höfuðbeinum

Word List (English to Old Norse)

English	Old Norse
healthy	heill
heard	heyrðu
held	helt
Helga (name)	Helgu
help	björg
helpless	hlífarlauss
her	hana, hon
here	hér, hingat
hers	síns
hewed	hjuggust
hill	hól, hólinn
him	hann, hans, honum, sín
himself	sér, sjálfr
his	hans, honum, sín, sína, sinn, sinnar, sinni, síns, sínu, sínum
his-hand	hendinni
Hof	hofs
Hof (place)	Hofi, Hofs
hold	halds
hold-fulfil	haldkvæmara
home	heim, heima, heiman
honour	drengskap, virðingu
horse	hesti, hestr
horse-boy	hestasvein
horse-fight	hesta-ats, hestaþingi, hesta-þinginu
horse-house	hesthúsinn, hrossahúsi, hrossahússins
horse-man	hrossamaðr
horses	hesta, hestana, hestum, hestunum, hrossa, hrossin
horse-staffs	hestastafnum
hospitality	vist
house	húss
how	hvernig
how-many	hversu

I, i

English	Old Norse
I	ek, mér
I-am	ek
if	ef
ill	illt
in	á, í, inn, við
injury	sárunum
inside	inn
intended	ætluðu
into	í
invited	bauð
is	er, sé
is-it	er
it	at, hon, þat, þat
it, that, to	at

J, j

English	Old Norse
jaw	skoltinn
Jon (name)	Jóns
journey	ferð
joyful	feginn
judging	dœmi

K, k

English	Old Norse
keep-secret	leyna
killed	drepit, veginn, vegit
Killer-Bjarni (name)	Víga-Bjarna
killing	vig
kinsmen	frændi, frændum
knees	kné
knew	víst
know	kann, kenni, veit, vita, vitum
known	vita
Kolbein (name)	Kolbeinn

L, l

English	Old Norse
laid	lágði, lagðist
lambs-heads	lambahöfuðin
last	siðara
lawspeaker	lögsögumaðr
lay	lá
laying	lægi
life	æfi, ævi, fjörsins
likeliest	liklegastir
listen	hlýða

Word List (English to Old Norse)

English	Old Norse
little	litlu, lítt
live	lifir, liflr
lived	bjó
looked	leit
looked-after	varðveitti
look-for	leita
looking-for	leita
loose	lausir
luck	happi

M, m

English	Old Norse
Magnus (name)	Magnus, Magnúsar, Magnúss
make	gerir
man	maðr, mann, manns
man's	manns
many	marga, margir, margt, mörgum
married	átti
matched	maki, öttu
may	má, mætta
may-be	megi
me	mér, mik, min
meadow	garðinu
meet	meta, mik
men	manna, menn
mercy	vægt
met	hitta, hitti, mér
mid-morning	dagmálum
might	mætta
mind	skapi
mine	mín, mína, mínir, minn, minni, mínum
miserable	armastr
misfortune	ógæfa
mishap	óhapp
mislaid	forlagðir
misplaced	mislagðar
miss	missa
mood	skap
more	meira, meirr
more-powerful	rikara
morning	morgun, morguninn
most	mesti

English	Old Norse
mother-of	móðir, móður
mourn	sýta
mouths	hváftana
move	bregð
much	mikit, miklar, miklir, miklu, mjök
my	minnar, mínum
myself	mér, sjálfr

N, n

English	Old Norse
named	heitir, hét, nefndr
near	nær
neck	hála
need	þurfa
needs	þarf
never	aldregi
news	tiðast, tíðast, tíðinda
noble	riks, skörugligast
none	eigi, engan, engi, engir, öngu
no-one	engi
nor	né
not	eigi, ekki
not-be	eigi
nothing	engi, engis
not-used-to	óvanari
now	nú

O, o

English	Old Norse
of	á, af, af, of
off	af
often	oft, oftar
of-the-other	annarrar
of-you	afþér, yður
Ogmund (name)	Ögmundar
old	gamall
older	ellri
old-man	karl
on	á, í
one	annarr, eina, einn, einum, gott
one-thing	eitt

Word List (English to Old Norse)

English	Old Norse
only	eigu, engis
or	eðr
orderly	stilltr
Orm (name)	Orms
other	aðrir, annarra, öðrum
our	várir
out	út, útan, úti
outlaw	skógarmaðr
outlawed	skógarmaðrinn
out-of	ör
outside	út, úti
outstanding-man	afbragðsmaðr
out-travel	útan
over	ofan, yfir
overcome	bart

P, p

part	hlut
pass	leið
passed	líðr
paupers	framfœrslumenn
peace	kyrt
penalty	víti
people	mann, menn
people's	manna
persistent	þrautbeztr
place	stað
pledge	handsöl
popular	vinsælli
powerful	öflugr
praise	hrósit
prepared	búit, býr
prestigious-people	stórmenna
promise	lofa
promises	heit
protection	hiífar
provisions	vist
pulled	togat
purchase	kaup
pushed	stakk

R, r

ram-heads	geldinga-höfuð
ran	hleypr, hljóp, rann
Rannveig (name)	Rannveig
rather	heldr, helzt
refer	vísar
reins	taumana
reported	títt
rested	hvílir
revenge	hefna
ride	reið
riding-horses	reiðhesta
risk	hætta
Rome-city (place)	Rúmaborg
rose	reis, rísa

S, s

said	kvað, kváðust, mælti, sagði, sagði, segir
said-too-much	ofmælt
sake	sakir, sóknum
same-district	samheraðs
sat	sæti, sat, sátu
saw	sá, visar
say	mæl, segi, segir
scared	hræddr
see	sé
seeing-little	sjónlitill
seem	þykkir
seemed	þykkir
seeming	þykkir
seems	sýnist, þykki, þykkir
seens	þykkir
self-supported	sjálfbjarga
sent	sendi
seriously	alvöru
servant	húskarl
servants	húskarla, húskarlar
serves-you-right	makligleikum
settle	bústú, sitja
shaking	skelfr

Word List (English to Old Norse)

English	*Old Norse*	*English*	*Old Norse*
shall	man, mant, mun, skal, skalt, skaltú	spoke-of	mæltu
		sport	leik
shall-you	muntú, skaltú	Staff-Struck (name)	Stangarhögg, Stangarhöggs
sharpened	hvatti		
she	hon	stain	flekk
sheep-heads	dilka-höfuð	stand	standa, stoða
shield	skjöldinn, skjöldr	standing	stendr
shields	skjöldu	Stein (name)	Steins
ship	skip	stepped	sté
shirts	skyrtum	still	enn, kyrt
shirt-sheet	skyrtublaði	stood	stóð
shoe-thongs	skóþvengir	stoop	bograt
short	skamt	stooped	lýtr
short-sword	sax, saxi, saxinu	straightaway	þegar
should	man, mantú, mun, skyldi, skyldu	stream	lœkjarins
		strength	þrek
should-be	skyldi	strike	höggva
Siðu-Hallson (name)	Siðu-Hallsson	striking	högg
sight-less	sjónlausum	stronger	ríkar
Sighvat (name)	Sighvats	struck	hjó, höggr, laust, lostinn, lýstr
Sigrid (name)	Sigríði		
silence	þagat	struggle	þraut
since	því	stud-horses	stóðhross
singe	svíða, sviðit	stupid	heimskr
single-combat	einvigis, einvígis	submit	undir
situated	siti	such	slika, slíka, slíkt, slikum
Skegg-Broddi (name)	Skegg-Broddi	summer	sumar
sleep	svefns	Sunnudal (place)	Sunnudal
slept	sofa	support	stoðar
slipped	runnit	suppose	ætla, ætlar, ætlum
Snorri (name)	Snorra	surprised	kynlegt
so	sá, svá	Sutri (place)	Valería
sold	seldu	Svinafellings (name)	Svínfellings
some	nökkura, nökkurum	sword	sverð, sverðit
somewhat	nökkuru		
son	son, sonar, sonr, syni		
son-death	sonar-dauðinn		

T, t

English	*Old Norse*
son's	sonar
south	suðr
spare	spara	take	tak, taka
speak	mæla, mælast, mælir	takes	taka, tekr
speaking	mælt	taking	tókum
speedily	snarligra	talk	tals
spirit	dugi	talking	talat, tali
spoke	mælti	taunted	kals
spoken	mælt	taunting	frýju-orð
		tell	seg, segi, segja

Word List (English to Old Norse)

English	Old Norse	English	Old Norse
tell-you	teljast	this	í, þat, þenna, þess, þessarra, þessu, þessum, þetta, þit
than	at, enn, er		
that	at, er, sú, það, þat, þetta	Thora (name)	Þórn, Þóru
		Thorarin (name)	Þŏrarinn, Þórarinn, Þórarins
the	hinn		
the-assembly	þings	Thord (name)	Þórð, Þórðar, Þórðr
the-bishop	biskups	Thordis (name)	Þórdísar
the-blind	blinda	Thord's (name)	Þórðar
the-blow	höggvið	Thorgeir (name)	Þórgeirs
the-blows	höggunum	Thorgrim's (name)	Þórgríms
the-chieftain	góða	Thorhall (name)	Þórhall, Þórhallr
the-day	dag	Thorid (name)	Þuriðar
the-district	heraðinu	Thorkatla (name)	Þórkatla
the-earl	jarls	Thorstein (name)	Þŏrsteinn, Þórstein, Þórsteini, Þórsteinn, Þórsteins
the-hill	hölinn, höllinn		
the-horse	best		
the-horses	hestarnir, hrossa	Thorstein's (name)	Þórsteini, Þórsteins
their	þeim, þeira, þeiri	Thorvald (name)	Þórvald, Þórvaldr
theirs	sína, sínum	those	þeim, þeira
the-killing	vigit	though	þo, þó, þótt
them	þeim	thought	hugða, hugði, mundi, þótti, þykkjast
the-man	maðr, maðrinn		
themselves	sér	thoughts	hug
then	enn, hit, síðan, þá, þau	thralls	þræla
the-night	nóttina	three	þriggja, þrjá
the-old-man	karl, karls	thrives	þriflst
the-other	öðrum	through	gegnum
the-priest	prests	tie	bind
there	hingat, þær, þar, þefri, þeiri, til	tied	bindr
		time	stundu
therefore	því	to	á, at, í, til, tíl
the-sagas	sögur	to-be	at
the-saga-tale	sögu-þætti	to-do	tilgert
the-same	sama	together	saman
the-Sturlusons (name)	Sturlusona	to-give	veita
the-sword	sverðit	to-go	fara
the-table	borð, borði	to-invite	bjóða
the-tables	borða	to-lay	leggja
the-wicked	glœp	told	sagði, sagt, segir, segja, talat
the-woman	kona, konan		
they	hinir, þau, þeir, þeira	tolerate	þoli
they-are	eru	to-me	mér, mik
think	þykki, þykkir	tongue	tungu, tungunni
thirsty	þyrstir	took	taka, tekr, tók
		torso	bolinn
		to-think	þykkja

43

Word List (English to Old Norse)

English	Old Norse
to-travel	fara
toughness	harðfengi
towards	móti, til
to-you	sér, þér
Travel	far, fara, ferr
travelled	fara, ferr, fœra, fór
trolls	troll
true	
true	
true-man	trú-maðr
truth	trútt
two	tvá

U, u

English	Old Norse
under	undir
un-equal-man	ójafnaðar
un-gift	ógifta
unremarkable	ómjúkir
until	til, unz
up	upp, uppá
up-to	undir
us	okkr, oss

V, v

English	Old Norse
valour	hreysti
valued	virðir
viking	víkingr

W, w

English	Old Norse
wake	vekja
want	vant
wanted	nenta
warily	varlega
warn	varnaði
warriors	kappi
was	er, væri, var, varð
was-named	hét
we	oss, vér
weak	seint
weapon	vápn

English	Old Norse
weapons	vápn, vápna
weapons-exchange	vápnaskiftum
we-are	vér
wear-out	slita
weeping	gráta
well	vel
went	fara, fœri, fór, ganga, gekk, gengi, gengr, gengu
were	eru, var, váru
were-you	vartú
what	er, hvat, hvert
when	enn, er, hvenær
where	er, hvar
whether	hvárt
which	er, hvert, sem, því
who	er, hverr
who-are	er
why	hverr, hvi
widely	víða
will	valdi, vilda, vilja, vill, vilt
willed	vildi
win	vinna
winter	vetrinn
wish	vil, vilda, vilit, vilja, vilt
with	er, með, við, vit
without	ómegð
without-cause	saklausa
without-revenge	óhefnt
wits	vits
woman	konu
women	konum, konur, kvenna
wonder	kynlegt
worded	orðit
words	orð, orða, orðit, orðum
work	verk, verks
worked	vann
working	forverka
worse	verr, verra
worst	verr
worth	verðr
worthiness	virðingu
worthy	svivirðing

Word List (English to Old Norse)

English	Old Norse
would	mant, munda, mundak, mundi, mundir, mundu, mundum, muni, væri, vildi
would-be	vara

Y, y

Yngvild (name)	Ingveldr
Yngvild's (name)	Ingveldra
you	þér, þik, þín, þínu, þínum, þú, yðr
young	ungum
yours	sitt, þín, þína, þinn, þíns, þínum
youth	œsku
you-two	þér
Yule (name)	Jól

The Tale of Thorstein Staff-Struck (*Old Icelandic*)

Old Icelandic	Literal	English
1	**1**	**1**
Maður hét Þórarinn er bjó í Sunnudal, gamall maður og sjónlítill.	A-man was-named Thorarin who lived in Sunnudal, old man and seeing-little.	There was a man named Thorarin who lived in Sunnudal, he was an old man and nearly blind.
Hann hafði verið rauðavíkingur í æsku sinni.	He had been fierce-viking in youth his.	He had been a fierce viking in his youth.
Hann var eigi dældarmaður þótt hann væri gamall.	He was not gentle-man though he was old.	He was not a gentle man even though he was old.
Son átti hann sér einn er Þorsteinn er nefndur.	A-son had he himself one who Thorstein was named.	He had a son who was named Thorstein.
Hann var mikill maður og öflugur og vel stilltur og vann svo fyrir búi föður síns að eigi mundi þriggja verk manna annarra hallkvæmara.	He was great man and powerful and well composed and worked so for estate father his that not could three work men other hold-fulfil.	He was a great and powerful man and well composed, and he worked so hard on his father's estate that three other men could not fulfil.
Þórarinn var heldur félítill maður en vel margt átti hann vopna.	Thorarin was rather fee-little man but well many had he weapons.	Thorarin was rather a poor man but he had many weapons.
Þeir áttu og stóðhross feðgar og var þeim það helst til fjár er þeir seldu undan hestana því að engir brugðust að reið né hug.	They had also stud-horses father-and-son and was their that rather to fee that they sold away horses because that none broke to ride nor spirit.	They also had some stud horses and that was their main source of wealth, for the horses they sold were not broken by riding nor broken in spirit.
Þórður er maður nefndur.	Thord was a-man named.	There was a man named Thord.
Hann var húskarl Bjarna frá Hofi.	He was servant Bjarni's from Hof.	He was a servant of Bjarni from Hof.
Hann varðveitti reiðhesta Bjarna því að hann var kallaður hrossamaður.	He looked-after riding-horses Bjarni's accordingly that he was called horse-man.	He looked after Bjarni's riding-horses and was therefore called horse-man.
Þórður var ójafnaðarmaður mikill og lét hann marga þess og kenna er hann var ríkismanns húskarl.	Thord was un-equal-man much and had he many this and be-known that he was noble-man's servant.	Thord was very much an arrogant man and he had it known that he was a nobleman's servant.

The Tale of Thorstein Staff-Struck (Old Icelandic)

Old Icelandic	Literal	English
En eigi var hann sjálfur að meira verður og eigi varð hann að vinsælli.	But not was he himself the more worth and not was he that popular.	But this did not add to his worth or his popularity.
Þeir menn voru enn á vist með Bjarna er annar hét Þórhallur en annar Þorvaldur.	They men were then in hospitality with Bjarni who one named Thorhall and another Thorvald.	There were then men staying with Bjarni, one was named Thorhall, and another Thorvald.
Þeir voru uppaustrarmenn miklir um allt það er þeir heyrðu í héraði.	They were gossipers much about all that which they heard in the-district.	They were very much gossipers about all that the heard in the district.
Þeir Þorsteinn og Þórður mæltu til hestaats ungum hestum.	They Thorstein and Thord spoke-of to horse-fight young horses.	Thorstein and Thord spoke about a horse fight for their young horses.
Og er þeir öttu þá vildi hestur Þórðar verr bítast.	And when they matched then would horse Thord's worst bite.	And when they fought, Thord's horse was bitten the worst.
Þórður lýstur nú á skoltinn hesti Þorsteins er honum þótti sinn hestur verr hafa, mikið högg.	Thord struck now to jaw horse Thorstein's when he thought his horse worse had, much been-struck.	Thord now struck the jaw of Thorstein's horse when he realised that his horse had been struck worse.
En Þorsteinn sá það og lýstur á móti hest Þórðar heldur meira högg og rann nú hesturinn Þórðar og æptu menn þá með kappi.	Then Thorstein saw that and struck to towards the-horse Thord's rather more striking and ran now horse Thord's and called-out men then with warriors.	Then Thorstein saw that and struck at Thord's horse rather more, and Thord's horse backed away, and then the warriors who were with them called out.
Þá lýstur Þórður Þorstein með hestastafnum og kom á brúnina og hljóp hún ofan fyrir augað.	Then struck Thord Thorstein with horse-staffs and came to eyebrow and ran it over before eye.	Then Thord struck Thorstein with his horse staff which came to his eyebrow and ran over his eye.
Þá risti Þorsteinn af skyrtublaði sínu og bindur upp brúnina og lætur sem ekki hafi að orðið og biður að menn leyni þessu föður hans.	Then carved Thorstein off shirt-sheet his and bound up eyebrow and behaved as-if not had which worded and asked that people keep-secret this father his.	Then Thorstein carved from his shirt and bandaged his eyebrow and behaved thus that he did not say anything about it, and he asked people to keep this a secret from his father.
Og féll þetta þar nú niður.	And fell that there now down.	And the matter fell down there.

The Tale of Thorstein Staff-Struck (Old Icelandic)

Old Icelandic	Literal	English
Þeir Þorvaldur og Þórhallur höfðu þetta fyrir kallsi og kölluðu hann Þorstein stangarhögg.	They Thorvald and Thorhall had this before taunted and called him Thorstein Staff-Struck.	Thorvald and Thorhall has thus taunted him and called him Thorstein Staff-Struck.
Litlu fyrir jól um veturinn risu konur til verks í Sunnudal.	Little before Yule about winter rose women to work in Sunnudal.	A little before Yule in winter when women got up to work in Sunnudal.
Þá stóð Þorsteinn og upp og bar inn hey og lagðist síðan niður í bekk.	Then stood Thorstein and got-up and carried in hay and laid then down on bench.	Then Thorstein got up and carried some hay inside and then lay down on a bench.
Nú kemur Þórarinn karl innar, faðir hans, og spurði hver þar lægi.	Now came Thorarin old-man in, father his, and asked why there laying.	Now Thorarin his father, an old man, came in and asked him why he was laying there.
Þorsteinn sagði til sín.	Thorstein said to him.	Thorstein told him.
"Hví ertu svo snemma á fótum sonur?"	"Why are-you so early about feet son?"	"Why are you up on your feet so early, son?",
sagði Þórarinn karl.	said Thorarin old-man.	said Thorarin the old man.
Þorsteinn svarar:	Thorstein answered:	Thorstein answered:
"Við fá þykir mér að meta það sem hér er að vinna",	"With few seems to-me to meet that which here is to win",	"With few it seems to me that might help me here",
sagði Þorsteinn.	said Thorstein.	said Thorstein.
"Er þér ekki illt í höfuðbeinunum sonur?"	"Are you not ill in head-bone son?"	"Are you not ill in the head, son?",
kvað Þórarinn karl.	said Thorarin old-man.	said the old man.
"Eigi kenni eg þess",	"Not know I this",	"Not that I have noticed",
sagði Þorsteinn.	said Thorstein.	said Thorstein.
"Hvað segir þú mér sonur af hestaþinginu því er í fyrra sumar var? Varstu ekki lostinn í svíma frændi sem hundur?"	"What say you to-me son of horse-fight which that in before summer was? Were-you not struck to dizziness kinsmen as a-dog?"	What can you tell me about the horse fight last summer? Were you not struck dizzy by your kinsmen like a dog?"
"Engi þykir mér virðing í vera",	"Nothing seems to-me worthy to be",	"It is not worthy to me",

The Tale of Thorstein Staff-Struck (Old Icelandic)

Old Icelandic	Literal	English
sagði Þorsteinn, "að kalla það heldur högg en atburð".	said Thorstein, "to call that rather striking than accident".	said Thorstein, "to call it rather a blow than an incident".
Þórarinn mælti:	Thorarin said:	Thorarin said:
"Ekki mundi mig þess vara að eg mundi ragan son eiga".	"Not thought me this would-be that I would cowardly son have".	"Not would this be to me, that I would have a coward son".
"Mæl þú það eitt um nú faðir",	"Say you that one-thing about now father",	"Tell me one thing about now, father",
sagði Þorsteinn, "er þér þykir eigi ofmælt síðar".	said Thorstein, "that you seem not or-speaking afterwards".	said Thorstein, "which you do not think is said-too-much later".
"Ekki mun eg hér svo mikið um mæla",	"Not shall I here so much about speak",	"I will not speak so much here",
sagði Þórarinn, "sem mér er að skapi".	said Thorarin, "as to-me is to mind".	said Thorarin, "of what I am in the mood to say".

2

Nú reis Þorsteinn upp og tók vopn sín og gekk síðan heiman og fór uns hann kom til hrossahúss þess er Þórður gætti hesta Bjarna í og var hann þar fyrir.	Now rose Thorstein up and took weapon his and went afterwards home and travelled until he came to horse-house this that Thord guarded horses Bjarni's in and was he there before.	Now Thorstein got up and took his weapon, and then went away from home, and went until he came to the horse-house where Thord looked after Bjarni's horses, and he was there before.
Þá hittir Þorsteinn Þórð og mælti til hans:	Then found Thorstein Thord and spoke to him:	Then Thorstein met Thord, and said to him,
"Vita vildi eg það Þórður minn hvort það varð þér voðaverk er eg fékk af þér högg í fyrra sumar á hestaþingi eða hefir það að vilja þínum orðið og hvort bæta muntu þá vilja yfir".	"Know wish I that Thord me whether that was you accident that I got of you a-strike in before summer at horse-fight or have that to wish you words and whether compensation you-should then will over".	"I wish to know, my Thord, whether it was a tragedy to you when I was beaten by you last summer at a horse meeting, or whether it has been at your will, and whether you will make amends for it".
Þórður svarar:	Thord answered:	Thord answered:

The Tale of Thorstein Staff-Struck (Old Icelandic)

Old Icelandic	Literal	English
"Ef þú átt tvo hvoftana þá bregð þú tungunni sitt sinn í hvorn og kalla í öðrum voðaverk ef þú vilt en í öðrum kalla þú alvöru.	"If you had two mouths then move you tongue yours that in each and call in the-other an-accident if you wish but in the-other call you seriously.	"If you had two mouths, then you could move your tongue into each and call it either an accident if you wish but in another call it serious.
Og eru það nú bæturnar þær er þú munt af mér fá".	And are-you that now compensation there that you shall of me get".	And now those are the benefits you'll get from me".
"Búst þú þá svo við",	"Settle you then so with",	"Settle with that as you will",
sagði Þorsteinn,	said Thorstein,	said Thorstein,
"að vera má að eg heimti eigi oftar".	"to be may that I claim not often".	"it may be that I don't make this claim often".
Síðan hleypur Þorsteinn að honum og höggur Þórð banahögg, gekk síðan til húss að Hofi og hitti úti konu eina og mælti við hana:	Then ran Thorstein at him and struck Thord death-blow, went afterwards to house at Hof and met outside woman one and spoke with her:	Then Thorstein ran at him and stuck Thord his death-blow, and went afterwards to the house at Hof and met a woman outside and spoke with her:
"Seg þú Bjarna að naut hafi stangað Þórð hestasvein hans og mun hann bíða þar til þess er hann kemur hjá hestahúsinu".	"Tell you Bjarni that bull has gored Thord horse-boy his and should he abide there to this that he comes beside". horse-house".	"Tell Bjarni that a bull has gored Thord horse-man, and he should wait there until he comes to the stable".
"Far þú heim maður",	"Travel you home man",	"Go back home, man",
sagði hún,	said she,	she said,
"en eg segi þá er mér sýnist".	"then I say then what to-me seems".	"and I will way when it seems to me to do so".
Nú fer Þorsteinn heim en konan fer til verks síns.	Now travelled Thorstein home and the-woman went to work hers.	Now Thorstein travelled home and the woman went to her work.

3

Bjarni reis upp um morguninn og er hann var undir borð kominn þá spurði Bjarni hvar Þórður væri og svöruðu menn að hann mundi til hrossa farinn.	Bjarni rose up about morning and as he was under the-table came then asked Bjarni where Thord was and answered people that he would to the-horses gone.	Bjarni got up that morning and was sitting at the table, then Bjarni asked where Thord was, and people answered that he would have travelled to the horses.

The Tale of Thorstein Staff-Struck (Old Icelandic)

Old Icelandic	Literal	English
"Heim hugði eg hann þó mundu kominn",	"Home thought I he though would come",	"I thought he would have come home",
kvað Bjarni,	said Bjarni,	said Bjarni,
"ef hann væri heill".	"if he was healthy".	"if he was well".
Þá tók kona til orða, sú er Þorsteinn hafði hitta:	Then took the-woman to words, that which Thorstein had met:	Then the woman that Thorsten had met took to words:
"Satt er það er oss er oft sagt konum að þar er lítið til vits að taka sem vér erum konur.	"True is that which we are often told women that there is little to wits to take which we are women.	"It is true what is told of us women, that there is little to wits taken as we are women.
Hér kom Þorsteinn stangarhögg í morgun, kvað naut hafa stangað Þórð svo að hann mundi eigi sjálfbjargi verða.	Here came Thorstein Staff-Struck in morning, said a-bull had gored Thord so that he would not self-supported be.	Thorstein Staff-Struck came here this morning, and said a bull had struck Thord so that he could not support himself.
En eg nennti eigi þá að vekja þig og þá hvarf mér úr hug síðan".	But I wanted not then to wake you and then disappeared to-me from thoughts afterwards".	But I didn't want to wake you, and then it disappeared from my thoughts afterwards".
Bjarni sté þá undan borði, gekk þá til hrossahússins og fann þar Þórð veginn og var hann síðan jarðaður.	Bjarni stepped then from-under the-table, went then to horse-house and found there Thord killed and was he afterwards earthed.	Bjarni stepped out from under the table, and then went to the stable and found Thord there killed, and he was buried afterwards.
Bjarni býr nú mál til og gerir Þorstein sekan um vígið.	Bjarni prepared now a-case towards and make Thorstein guilty about the-killing.	Bjarni now prepared a case to make Thorstein guilty of the killing.
En Þorsteinn sat heima í Sunnudal og vann fyrir föður sínum og lét Bjarni þó kyrrt vera.	Then Thorstein sat home in Sunnudal and worked for father his and had Bjarni though still be.	But Thorstein stayed at home in Sunnudal and worked for his father, and Bjarni had little done though.
Um haustið sátu menn við sviðuelda að Hofi en Bjarni lá úti á eldahússveggnum og hlýddi þaðan til tals manna.	About autumn sat people with bonfires at Hof when Bjarni lay out on fire-house-wall and followed from there talk people's.	About autumn the people of Hof had bonfires, and Bjarni lay outside on the fire-house-wall and followed other people's talking.
Nú taka þeir bræður til orða, Þórhallur og Þorvaldur:	Now took they brothers to words, Thorhall and Thorvald:	Now the brothers Thorhall and Thorvald took to words:

The Tale of Thorstein Staff-Struck (Old Icelandic)

Old Icelandic	Literal	English
"Eigi varði oss þess þegar vér tókum vist með Víga-Bjarna að vér mundum hér svíða dilkahöfuð en Þorsteinn skógarmaður hans skyldi svíða geldingahöfuð.	"Not expected us this when we- are taking provisions with Killer-Bjarni that we would here singe sheep-heads when Thorstein outlaw his should singe ram-heads.	"We did not expect when we came to stay with Killer-Bjarni that we would be here singing sheeps" heads when Thorstein the outlaw would be singing rams' heads.
Væri eigi verra að hafa meir vægt frændum sínum í Böðvarsdal og sæti nú eigi skógarmaðurinn jafnhátt honum í Sunnudal.	Would not-be worse than have more mercy kinsmen his in Bodvarsdale and sat now not outlawed equally him in Sunnudal.	It would not have been worse to have his merciful kinsmen in Bodvarsdale and not sat equally with the outlaw in Sunnudal.
En lagðir verða forlagðir ef fyrir sárunum verða og eigi vitum vér hvenær hann vill þenna flekk má af virðingu sinni".	But had become mislaid if before injury comes and not know we when he will this stain may of worthiness his".	But what is laid becomes mislaid when it becomes faced with injury, and we don't know when he will off this stain from his honour".
Maður einn svaraði:	Man one answered:	One man answered:
"Slíkt er verr mælt en þagað og líklegt að ykkur hafi tröll togað tungu úr höfði.	"Such is worse spoken than silence and likely that you have trolls pulled tongue out-of head.	"Such that is spoken is worse than silence, and it's likely that the trolls pulled the tongue out of your head.
Ætlum vér að hann nenni eigi að taka björg frá föður hans sjónlausum og annarri ómegð þeirri sem í Sunnudal er.	Suppose we that he bothers not to take help from father his sight-less and another without there as in Sunnudal at.	We think that he does not bother to take help from his blind father and other dependants there at Sunnudal.
En kynlegt þykir mér ef þið svíðið oft lambahöfuðin hér eða hrósið því hvað í Böðvarsdal var títt".	About surprised think I if you-two singe often lambs-heads here or praise therefore what in Bodvarsdale was reported".	But I will be surprised if you two singe many more lamb's heads here, or talk about what happened at Bodvarsdale".
Nú fara menn til borða og síðan til svefns og fann ekki á Bjarna hvað talað hafði verið.	Now travelled men to-the-tables and then to sleep and found not of Bjarni what told had been.	Now the people went to the tables and then to sleep and Bjarni gave nothing away of what had been told.

4

Um morguninn vakti Bjarni þá Þórhall og Þorvald og bað þá ríða í Sunnudal og færa sér höfuð Þorsteins við bolinn skilið að dagmálum	About morning awoke Bjarni then Thorhall and Thorvald and asked then to-ride to Sunnudal and travelled themselves head Thorstein's with torso divided that mid-morning	About morning Bjarni woke Thorhall and Thorvald and asked them to ride to Sunnudal and bring Thorstein's severed head divided from its torso by mid-morning

The Tale of Thorstein Staff-Struck (Old Icelandic)

Old Icelandic	Literal	English
"og þykir mér þið", sagði hann, "líklegastir til að færa flekk af virðingu minni ef eg hefi ekki þrek til sjálfur".	"and seems to-me you", said he, "likeliest to that bring stain of worthiness mine if I have not strength to myself".	"and it seems to me that you", he said, "will bring the stain off my honour if I have not the strength to myself".
Nú þykjast þeir víst ofmælt hafa og fara þeir nú þó uns þeir koma í Sunnudal.	Now thought they knew said-too-much had and travelled they now though until they came to Sunnudal.	Now they thought that they had said too much, but they travelled until they came to Sunnudal.
Þorsteinn stóð í durum og hvatti sax.	Thorstein stood in doorway and sharpened short-sword.	Thorstein stood in the doorway and sharpened a short-sword.
Og er þeir komu þar þá spurði hann hvert þeir ætluðu	And as they came there then asked he what they intended	And as they came he asked them what their intentions were,
en þeir sögðust hrossa leita skyldu	then they said horses looking-for should	and they said that they were looking for some horses,
en Þorsteinn kvað þeirra mundu skammt að leita, "er hér eru við garð".	then Thorstein said they would short to look-for, "but here they-were with fences".	then Thorstein said that they would not have to look far "but they are here by the fence".
"Eigi er víst að við finnum hrossin ef þú vísar okkur eigi gerr til".	"Not is-it certain that with finding horses if you refer us not do to".	"It is not certain that we will find the horses if you do not refer us".
Þorsteinn gengur þá út.	Thorstein went then outside.	Then Thorstein went outside.
Og er þeir koma í garðinn ofan þá færir Þorvaldur upp öxina og hleypur að honum en Þorsteinn stakk við honum hendi sinni svo að hann féll fyrir.	And as they came to meadow across then brought Thorvald up axe and ran at him but Thorstein pushed against him arms his so that he fell before.	And as they went across the meadow, Thorvald brought up an axe and ran at him but Thorstein pushed against his arms so that he fell before him.
Þorsteinn lagði saxinu í gegnum hann.	Thorstein laid short-sword in through him.	Thorstein laid his short-sword through him.
Þá vildi Þórhallur veita honum tilræði og hafði hann slíka för sem Þorvaldur.	Then willed Thorhall to-give him assault and had he such for as Thorvald.	Then Thorhall wished to assault him, and he had the same as Thorvald.
Þá bindur Þorsteinn á bak báða þá og lætur upp taumana á háls hestinum og vísar á leið öllu saman og ganga hestarnir nú heim til Hofs.	Then tied Thorstein to back both then and had up reins to neck horses and saw to pass all together and went the-horses now home to Hof.	Then Thorstein tied both back and had the reins up to the horses necks and saw them off together, an the horses went home to Hof.

The Tale of Thorstein Staff-Struck (Old Icelandic)

Old Icelandic	Literal	English
Húskarlar voru úti að Hofi og gengu inn og sögðu Bjarna að þeir Þorvaldur voru heim komnir og sögðu þá eigi erindlaust farið hafa.	Servants were out at Hof and went in and told Bjarni that they Thorvald were home coming and told then not errand-lost gone had.	The servants were outside at Hof and went in and told Bjarni that Thorvald and Thorhall had come home, and said that their errand had not gone in vain.
Gengur nú Bjarni út og sér nú hvernig um er búið og hefir ekki orða um fleira,	Went now Bjarni out and himself now how about was prepared and have not words about more,	Now Bjarni went out himself about what had happened, and had no more words about it, and had them buried.
lætur nú jarða þá. Og er nú kyrrt allt uns jól líður.	had now buried then. And was now peace all until Yule passed.	And it was now all peaceful until Yule had passed.

5

Þá tekur Rannveig til orða einn aftan er þau komu í sæng sína, Bjarni og hún:	Then took Rannveig to words one evening when they came to bed theirs, Bjarni and her:	Then Rannveig spoke one evening when her and Bjarni came to their bed:
"Hvað ætlar þú að nú sé tíðast talað í héraðinu?"	"What suppose you that now is news talking in-the-district?"	"What do you suppose people are talking about in the district?"
kvað hún.	said she.	she said.
"Eigi veit eg",	"Not know I",	"I do not know",
sagði Bjarni.	said Bjarni.	said Bjarni.
"Margir þykja mér ómerkir í sínum orðum", sagði hann.	"Many think me unremarkable in their words", said he.	"I think many of their words are unremarkable", he said.
"Það er nú tíðast að ræða að menn þykjast eigi vita hvað Þorsteinn stangarhögg mun þess gera að þér muni þurfa þykja að hefna.	"This is now news that discussing that people consider not known what Thorstein Staff-Struck would this do that you would need to-think to revenge.	"This is now what people are talking about, they think they don't know what Thorstein Staff-Struck would have to do for you to take revenge.
Hefir hann nú vegið húskarla þína þrjá.	Has he now killed servants yours three.	He has now killed three of your servants.
Þykir þingmönnum þínum eigi vænt til halds þar sem þú ert ef þessa er óhefnt og eru þér mjög mislagðar hendur í kné".	Think assembly-men yours not expect to hold there as you are if this is without-revenge and are your much misplaced hands on knees".	Your assembly-men do not expect to stay here as you are, if this is without revenge, and you have misplaced your hands on your knees.

The Tale of Thorstein Staff-Struck (Old Icelandic)

Old Icelandic	Literal	English
Bjarni svarar:	Bjarni answered:	Bjarni answered:
"Nú kemur hér að því sem mælt er að engi lætur sér annars víti að varnaði en hlýða mun eg þér hvað er þú mælir.	"Now comes here that since which spoken is that no-one has himself another's penalty to warn but listen should I to-you what is you speak.	"Now it comes to what is said, that no one gives himself another's misfortune as a warning, but I will obey you what you say.
Hefir Þorsteinn og fá saklausa drepið".	Has Thorstein and had without-cause killed".	Thorstein has killed few without cause".
Hætta þau þessu tali og sofa af um nóttina.	Concluded then this talking and slept of about the-night.	Then their talking concluded and they slept through the night.
Um morguninn vaknar Rannveig er Bjarni tók ofan skjöld sinn og spurði hún hvert hann skyldi.	About morning awoke Rannveig as Bjarni took down shield his and asked her where he should-be.	In the morning Rannveig woke up when Bjarni took down his shield and she asked where he was going.
Hann svarar:	He answered:	He answered:
"Nú skal skipta virðingu með okkur Þorsteini í Sunnudal",	"Now shall exchange honour between us Thorstein in Sunnudal",	"Now we shall exchange honour between us, Thorstein in Sunnudal",
segir hann.	said he.	he said.
"Hversu fjölmennur skaltu fara?"	"How-many followers shall travel?"	"How many followers shall you travel with?",
segir hún.	said she.	she said.
"Ekki mun eg draga fjölmenni að Þorsteini",	"Not shall I drag followers to Thorstein",	"I shall not drag followers to Thorstein",
segir hann,	said he,	he said,
"og mun eg einn fara".	"and shall I alone travel".	"and I shall travel alone".
"Gerðu eigi það",	"Do-you not that",	"Do not do that",
segir hún,	said she,	she said,
"að hætta þér einn undir vopn heljarmannsins".	"to risk to-you one up-to weapons cursed-man-this".	"to risk yourself alone up against the weapons of this cursed man".

The Tale of Thorstein Staff-Struck (Old Icelandic)

Old Icelandic	Literal	English
Bjarni mælti:	Bjarni spoke:	Bjarni spoke:
"Mun þér nú eigi verða þeirra kvenna dæmi er það gráta á annarri stundu er eggja á annarri? En eg þoli oft lengi frýjuorð bæði þér og öðrum en þá stoðar og ekki að letja mig þá er eg vil fara".	"Should you now not become those women judging who-are this weeping at another time who-are encouraging in another? But I tolerate often along taunting both of-you and others but then support and not to discourage me then as I wish to-go".	"Should you not now become one-of-those women who deem to weep at one moment but encourage at another? Before I have tolerated frequently and long enough the taunts of you and others, but then support me and not discourage me as I wish to go".
Bjarni fer nú í Sunnudal og stendur Þorsteinn í durum og köstuðust þeir á nokkurum orðum.	Bjarni went now to Sunnudal and standing Thorstein in doorway and exchanged they of some words.	Bjarni now went to Sunnudal and there was Thorstein standing in the doorway, and they exchanged some words.
Bjarni mælti:	Bjarni spoke:	Bjarni spoke:
"Þú skalt til einvígis ganga við mig í dag Þorsteinn á hól þenna er hér er í túni".	"You shall to single-combat go with me to day Thorstein on hill this which here is in field".	"You shall go to single combat with me today Thorstein, on this hill which is here in the field.
"Allt er mér til þess vant",	"All is me to this difficulty",	"This is all to my difficulty",
kvað Þorsteinn,	said Thorstein,	said Thorstein,
"að berjast við þig en eg skal þegar utan er skip ganga því að eg kann drengskap þinn að þú munt fá föður mínum forverk ef eg fer frá".	"to fight with you then I shall straightaway out-travel with ship going because that I know honour yours that you would give father mine for-work if I travel from".	"to fight with you, but I shall immediately travel out with the first ship going, because I know your honour, that you would give my father labour if I leave".
"Ekki stoðar nú undan að mælast",	"Not avail now from-under that speak",	"You cannot speak to avail yourself out from under this",
segir Bjarni.	said Bjarni.	said Bjarni.
"Leyfa muntu mér þá að eg finni föður minn áður",	"Allow shall-you for-me then that I find father mine before",	"Will you allow me that I can find my father before",
sagði Þorsteinn.	said Thorstein.	said Thorstein.
"Að vísu",	"To-be certain",	"Certainly",
sagði Bjarni.	said Bjarni.	said Bjarni.

The Tale of Thorstein Staff-Struck (Old Icelandic)

Old Icelandic	Literal	English
Þorsteinn gekk inn og sagði föður sínum að Bjarni var þar kominn og bauð honum til einvígis.	Thorstein went inside and told father his that Bjarni was there coming and invited him to single-combat.	Thorstein went inside and told his father that Bjarni was here and had invited him to single-combat.
Þórarinn karl svaraði:	Thorarin old-man answered:	Thorarin, the old man, answered:
"Von má hver maður þess vita ef hann á við sér ríkara mann og sitji samhéraðs honum og hafi þó gert honum nokkura ósæmd að hann mun eigi mörgum skyrtum slíta og kann eg því ekki að sýta þig að mér þykir þú mikið til hafa gert.	"Expect may any man this know if he to against himself more-powerful man and situated same-district his and has though done him some dishonour that he should not many shirts wear-out and know I therefore not to mourn you that to-me seems you much to have done.	"Any man may know to expect this, if he has done some discredit against a more powerful man in his own district, that he will not wear out many more shirts, and I know therefore not to mourn you because it seems to me that you have done much.
Tak nú vopn þín og ver þig sem skörulegast því að þar mundi verið hafa minnar ævi að ekki mundi eg bograð hafa fyrir slíkum sem Bjarni er. Er Bjarni þó hinn mesti kappi.	Take now weapons yours and be you as noble because that there would been have my life that not would I stoop have before such as Bjarni is. Is Bjarni though the most warrior.	Now take your weapons and be noble, because in my life I would not have stooped before such a man as Bjarni is. Even though he is the best warrior.
Þykir mér og betra að missa þín en eiga ragan son".	Consider I also better to miss you than own cowardly son".	I consider it better to lose you than to have a coward for a son".

6

Nú gengur Þorsteinn út og fara þeir síðan út á hólinn og taka til að berjast með harðfengi og hjuggust mjög hlífar fyrir hvorumtveggja.	Now went Thorstein out and went they afterwards out to the-hill and took to that fighting with toughness and hewed much protection before each-other.	Now Thorstein went outside and then they went out to the hill and took to fighting with toughness and struck down much of each other's shields.
Og þá er þeir höfðu mjög lengi barist þá mælti Bjarni til Þorsteins:	And then when they had much long carried then spoke Bjarni to Thorstein:	And then when they had carried on for a long time, Bjarni spoke to Thorstein:
"Þyrstir mig nú því að eg em óvanari erfiðinu en þú".	"Thirsty me now because that I am not-used-to difficulty as you".	"I am thirsty now because I am not used to such difficulty as you".
"Gakk þú þá til lækjarins",	"Go you then to stream",	"Then go to the stream",

The Tale of Thorstein Staff-Struck (Old Icelandic)

Old Icelandic	Literal	English
sagði Þorsteinn,	said Thorstein,	said Thorstein,
"og drekk".	"and drink".	"and drink".
Bjarni gerði svo og lagði niður sverðið hjá sér.	Bjarni did so and had downed the-sword beside himself.	Bjarni did so and put his sword down beside himself.
Þorsteinn tók upp, leit á og mælti:	Thorstein took up, looked at and spoke:	Thorstein took it up, looked at it, and spoke:
"Eigi mundir þú þetta sverð hafa í Böðvarsdal".	"Not would you this sword have at Bodvarsdale".	"You would not have had this sword at Bodvarsdale".
Bjarni svaraði engu.	Bjarni answered none.	Bjarni did not answer.
Ganga þeir nú upp á hólinn og berjast um stundar sakar	Went they now up the hill and fought about awhile's sake	Now they went up the hill and fought awhile,
og þykir Bjarna maðurinn vígkænn og þykir fastlegra fyrir en hann hugði.	and seemed Bjarni the-man battle-cunning and seemed fixed before than he thought.	and Bjarni seemed convinced that Thorstein was a cunning fighter and the fight seemed more fixed than before.
"Margt hendir mig nú í dag",	"Many happens to-me now this day",	"Everything is happening to me today",
sagði Bjarni,	said Bjarni,	said Bjarni,
"laus er nú skóþvengur minn".	"loose is now shoe-thongs mine".	"my shoe-thong is loose".
"Bind þú hann þá",	"Tie you it then",	"Then tie it",
kvað Þorsteinn.	said Thorstein.	said Thorstein.
Nú lýtur Bjarni niður en Þorsteinn gekk inn og hefir út skjöldu tvo og sverð eitt, gengur nú á hólinn til Bjarna og mælti við hann:	Now stooped Bjarni down then Thorstein went inside and had out shields two and sword one, went now to the-hill to Bjarni and spoke with him:	Now Bjarni stooped down and then Thorstein went inside and brought out two shields and one sword and went to the hill to Bjarni and spoke with him:
"Hér er skjöldur og sverð er faðir minn sendi þér og mun þetta eigi sljóvgast meir í höggunum en það sem þú hefir áður.	"Here is shield and sword that father mine sent you and should this not blunt more in the-blows than this which you had before.	"Here is a shield and sword that my father has sent you, and this should not be blunt with each blow like the sword you used before.

The Tale of Thorstein Staff-Struck (Old Icelandic)

Old Icelandic	Literal	English
Nenni eg og eigi að standa hlífarlaus lengur undir höggum þínum en gjarna vildi eg nú hætta þessum leik því að eg em hræddur að meira muni mega gæfa þín en ógifta mín og er hver frekur til fjörsins	Care I also not to stand helpless longer under blows yours and gladly will I now conclude this sport because that I am scared that more shall may-be gift yours than un-gift mine and that each eager to life	Also I do not care to stand helpless any longer under your blows and I would gladly conclude this sport because I am scared that your good luck shall be greater than my bad luck, and also each of us are eager to struggle to live,
um alla þraut ef eg mætti nokkuru um ráða".	about all struggle if I may somewhat about decide".	and I would if I could decide it".
"Eigi mun nú stoða að beiðast undan",	"Not should now stand to ask away-from",	"You should not try to ask your way out of it",
sagði Bjarni,	said Bjarni,	said Bjarni,
"berjast skal enn".	"fighting shall still".	"the fight must go on".
"Eigi mundi eg frekt höggva",	"Not would I eagerly strike",	"I wouldn't want to strike the first blow",
sagði Þorsteinn.	said Thorstein.	said Thorstein.
Þá höggur Bjarni allan skjöldinn af Þorsteini en þá hjó Þorsteinn skjöldinn af Bjarna.	Then struck Bjarni all shield of Thorstein's but then struck Thorstein shield of Bjarni's.	Then Bjarni struck and destroyed Thorstein's shield, and Thorstein struck and destroyed Bjarni's shield.
"Stórt er nú höggvið",	"Great is now the-blow",	"The striking is greater now",
kvað Bjarni.	said Bjarni.	said Bjarni.
Þorsteinn svaraði:	Thorstein answered:	Thorstein answered:
"Ekki hjóstu smærra högg".	"Not have-you-hit a-smaller blow".	"Your strike was no smaller".
Bjarni mælti:	Bjarni spoke:	Bjarni spoke:
"Betur bítur þér nú hið sama vopnið er þú hefir áður í dag haft".	"Better bite you now then the-same weapon than you have before in the-day had".	"Now it bites better than the same weapon that you had before in the day".
Þorsteinn mælti:	Thorstein spoke:	Thorstein spoke:

The Tale of Thorstein Staff-Struck (Old Icelandic)

Old Icelandic	Literal	English
"Spara mundi eg við mig óhapp ef eg mætti svo gera og berst eg hræddur við þig.	"Spare would I with me mishap if I might so do and fight I-am scared against you.	"I wish to spare myself from bad luck if I might do so, and I am scared to fight with you.
Vildi eg enn allt á þínu valdi vera láta".	Wish I then all to you will be had".	I wish for you to settle all of the matter".
Þá átti Bjarni að höggva og var nú hvortveggi hlífarlaus.	Then had Bjarni to strike and was now each helpless.	Then it was Bjarni's turn to strike and now each man was helpless.
Bjarni mælti þá:	Bjarni spoke then:	Then Bjarni spoke:
"Það mun illt kaup að taka glæp við miklu happi.	"It should ill purchase that takes the-wicked with much luck.	"It would ill afford to take much wickedness with luck.
Ætla eg mér fullgoldið fyrir þrjá húskarla mína þig einn ef þú vilt mér trúr vera".	Suppose I myself fully-golded for three servants mine you alone if you will to-me true be".	I would suppose myself fully paid for my three servants if you alone will serve me faithfully".
Þorsteinn sagði:	Thorstein said:	Thorstein said:
"Orðið hafa mér svo færi í dag á þér að eg mætti svíkja þig ef ógæfa mín gengi ríkara en lukka þín og mun eg eigi svíkja þig",	"Words have me so brought to day in you that I may betray you if misfortune mine went stronger than luck yours and should I not betray you",	"I have had many words with you today where I might have betrayed you if my misfortune was stronger than your luck, and so I will not betray you",
sagði Þorsteinn.	said Thorstein.	said Thorstein.
"Sé eg að þú ert afbragðsmaður", sagði Bjarni.	"See I that you are excellent-man", said Bjarni.	"I see now that you are an excellent man", said Bjarni.
"Lofa muntu mér að eg gangi inn til föður þíns",	"Promise shall-you me that I go inside to father yours",	"You will promise me that I go inside to your father",
sagði hann,	said he,	he said,
"og segja honum slíkt sem eg vil".	"and tell him such as I wish".	"and tell him about this as I wish".
"Gakk sem þú vilt fyrir mínum sökum",	"Go as you wish for my sake",	"Go as you wish, for my sake",
kvað Þorsteinn,	said Thorstein,	said Thorstein,
"og far þó varlega".	"and go though warily".	"and go carefully".

The Tale of Thorstein Staff-Struck (Old Icelandic)

Old Icelandic	*Literal*	*English*

7   7   7

Old Icelandic	Literal	English
Þá gekk og Bjarni að lokhvílu þeirri er Þórarinn karl lá í.	Then went also Bjarni to bed-closet there where Thorarin old-man lay in.	Then Bjarni went in to the bed closet where Thorarin the old man was laying.
Þórarinn spurði þá hver þar færi en Bjarni sagði til sín.	Thorarin asked then who there went then Bjarni told to him.	Thorarin then asked who went there and Bjarni told him.
"Hvað segir þú tíðinda Bjarni minn?"	"What say you news Bjarni mine?"	"What news do you speak about, my Bjarni?",
kvað Þórarinn.	said Thorarin.	said Thorarin.
"Víg Þorsteins sonar þíns",	"Killing Thorstein son yours",	"The killing of your son",
kvað Bjarni.	said Bjarni.	said Bjarni.
"Varðist hann nokkuð?"	"Defended he any-at-all?"	"Did he defend himself at all?",
kvað Þórarinn.	said Thorarin.	said Thorarin.
"Engan mann ætla eg snarlegra verið hafa í vopnaskipti en Þorstein son þinn".	"None man suppose I speedily been have I weapons-exchange than Thorstein son yours".	"I do not think I have been in such a speedy exchange of weapons as with your son Thorstein".
"Eigi er kynlegt að því",	"Not is wonder that therefore",	"It is no wonder therefore",
kvað karl,	said the-old-man,	said the old man,
"að þungt veitti við þig í Böðvarsdal er þú barst nú af syni mínum".	"that difficulty granted with you at Bodvarsdale that you overcome now of son mine".	"that you granted such difficulty to those at Bodvarsdale, that you have now overcome my son".
Þá mælti Bjarni:	Then spoke Bjarni:	Then Bjarni spoke:
"Eg vil bjóða þér til Hofs og skaltu sitja þar í öðru öndvegi meðan þú lifir og mun eg vera þér í sonar stað".	"I wish to-invite you to Hof and shall-you settle there in another foremost-seat as-long-as you live and should I be to-you in son's place".	"I wish to invite you to Hof, and you shall settle there in one of the foremost seats as long as you live, and I shall be in your son's place".
"Svo er mér farið",	"So is to-me going",	"So it goes to me",

The Tale of Thorstein Staff-Struck (Old Icelandic)

Old Icelandic	Literal	English
kvað karl,	said the-old-man,	said the old man,
"sem þeim er ekki eiga undir sér og verður heitum heimskur maður feginn.	"which those who not only submit to-you and worth called stupid man joyful.	"that those who do not alone accept you and your promise joyfully are stupid.
En svo eru heit yður höfðingja þá er þér viljið fróa manninn eftir slíka atburði að það er mánaðarfró en þá erum vér virðir eftir það sem aðrir framfærslumenn og fyrnast við það seint vorir harmar.	But so are promises of-you chieftains then that you wish console people after such events that it is a-month-from that then they-are we valued after it as other paupers and age with it weak our harm.	But so are the promises of you chieftains whom you wish to console after such events, that a month from then they are valued as paupers and their harm does not weaken with age.
En sá maður er handsöl tekur af slíkum manni sem þú ert má þó vel una sínum hlut hvað sem að dæma er.	Still so the-man who pledge takes of such man as you are may though well content with-his lot that which was deemed of.	Still, the man who takes a pledge with such a man as you may well be deemed to be content with his lot.
Mun eg og þessi handsöl taka af þér og gakk þú nú hingað til mín í rekkjugólfið og verður þú nær að ganga því að karl skelfur nú allur á fótum fyrir elli sakar og vanheilsu en eigi trútt að mér hafi eigi í skap runnið sonardauðinn".	Should I also this pledge take of you and come you now here to me in bed-closet and become you near to going because that old-man shaking now all on feet before age sake and failing-health but none truth to me has alone in mood slipped son-death".	So I should also take this pledge with you, and now come here to me in the bed closet and come nearer because I am an old man shaking on his feet for the sake of age and ill health, but one truth alone has caused my mood to slip, the death of my son".
Bjarni gekk nú í rekkjugólfið og tók í hönd Þórarni karli.	Bjarni went now into bed-closet and took in hand Thorarin the-old-man.	Bjarni now went into the bed closet and took Thorarin the old man's hand.
Hann fann þá að hann þuklaði á saxi og vildi þá leggja að Bjarna.	He found then that he felt a short-sword and willed then to-lay at Bjarni.	He then found that he felt a short sword that he wished to lay at Bjarni.
Hann kippti hendinni og mælti:	He dragged his-hand and spoke:	He drew his hand and spoke:
"Allra fretkarla armastur",	"All contemptible-man miserable",	"You are an all contemptible and miserable man",
sagði Bjarni.	said Bjarni.	said Bjarni.
"Nú mun að maklegleika fara með okkur.	"Now will it serve-you-right going between us.	"How it will serve you right what happens between us.

The Tale of Thorstein Staff-Struck (Old Icelandic)

Old Icelandic	Literal	English
Þorsteinn sonur þinn lifir og skal hann fara heim með mér til Hofs en þér skal fá þræla til forverks og skal þér einskis vant meðan þú lifir".	Thorstein son yours alive and shall he travel home with me to Hof and you shall get thralls to working and shall you nothing want as-long-as you live".	Thorstein your son is alive and he shall travel home with me to Hof, and you shall get servants to work for you and you shall want for nothing as long as you live".
Þorsteinn fór nú heim með Bjarna til Hofs og fylgdi honum allt til dauðadags og þótti nær einskis manns maki vera að drengskap og hreysti.	Thorstein travelled now home with Bjarni to Hof and followed him all until death-day and thought near only man matched had-been in honour and valour.	Now Thorstein travelled home with Bjarni to Hof and followed him in everything until the day he died, and he was thought the only man near to matching him in honour and valour.

8

Bjarni hélt vel virðingu sinni og var hann því vinsælli og betur stilltur sem hann var eldri og var allra manna þrautbestur og gerðist trúmaður mikill hinn síðasta hluta ævi sinnar.	Bjarni held well worthiness his and was he therefore popular and better orderly as he was older and were all men persistent and became true-man great the last part life his.	Bjarni held his standing well and became more popular and more self-controlled as he got older, and he was of all men the most persistent, and he became a great man of true faith for the last part of his life.
Bjarni fór utan og gekk suður og andaðist í þeirri ferð.	Bjarni travelled out and went south and died on their journey.	Bjarni travelled abroad and went south and died on that journey.
Hann hvílir í Borg þeirri er Vateri heitir og er það mikil Borg, skammt hingað frá Rómaborg.	He rested in Borg there was Sutri named and was that great Borg, short there from Rome-city.	He rested at a city that was named Sutri, and that was a great city, a short distance from the city of Rome.
Bjarni varð kynsæll maður.	Bjarni became kin-blessed man.	Bjarni became a man blessed with kin.
Hans sonur var Skegg-Broddi er víða kemur við sögur og var hinn mesti afbragðsmaður um sína daga.	His son was Skegg-Broddi who widely came in the-sagas and was the most outstanding-man about his day.	His son was Beard-Broddi who appears widely in the sagas, and he was the most outstanding man of his day.
Dóttir Bjarna hét Halla, móðir Guðríðar er Kolbeinn lögsögumaður átti.	Daughter Bjarni's named Halla, mother-of Gudrid who Kolbein lawspeaker married.	Bjarni had a daughter named Halla, the mother of Gudrid, who married Kolbein the lawspeaker.

The Tale of Thorstein Staff-Struck (Old Icelandic)

Old Icelandic	Literal	English
Yngvildur var og dóttir Bjarna er Þorsteinn Síðu-Hallsson átti og var þeirra sonur Magnús, faðir Einars, föður Magnúss biskups.	Yngvild was also daughter Bjarni's was Thorstein Sidu-Hallson married and was their son Magnus, father-of Einar, father-of Magnus the-bishop.	Bjarni had another daughter named Yngvild who married Thorstein Sidu-Hallson, their son was Magnus, the father of Einar, the father of Magnus the bishop.
Ámundi var og sonur Þorsteins og Yngvildar.	Amundi was also son Thorstein's and Yngvild's.	Thorstein and Yngvild also had a son named Amundi.
Hann átti Sigríði dóttur Þorgríms blinda.	He married Sigrid daughter Thorgrim's the-blind.	He married Sigrid, the daughter of Thorgrim the blind.
Hallfríður var og dóttir Ámunda, móðir Ámunda, föður Guðmundar, föður Magnúss goða og Þóru er Þorvaldur Gissurarson átti, og annarrar Þóru, móður Orms Svínfellings.	Hallfrid was also daughter Amundi's, mother Amundi's, father Gudmund's, father-of Magnus the-chieftain and Thora was Thorvald Gizurarson married, and of-the-other Thora, mother-of Orm Svinafellings.	Amundi also had a daughter named Hallfrid, the mother of Amundi, the father of Gudmund, the father of the chieftain Magnus, and of Thora who married Thorvald Gizurarson, and the other Thora who was the mother of Orm of Svinafell.
Guðrún var og Ámundadóttir, móðir Þórdísar, móður Helgu, móður Guðnýjar Böðvarsdóttur, móður Sturlusona, Þórðar og Sighvats og Snorra.	Gudrun was also Daughter-of-Amundi, mother-of Thordis, mother-of Helga, mother-of Gudny Daughter-of-Bodvar, mother-of The-Sturlusons, Thord and Sighvat and Snorri.	Amundi had another daughter called Gudrun, the mother of Thordis, the mother of Helga, the mother of Gudny Bodvar's daughter, the mother of the Sturlusons, Thord, Sighvat, and Snorri.
Rannveig var og Ámundadóttir, móðir Steins, föður Guðrúnar, móður Arnfríðar er Digur-Helgi átti.	Rannveig was also Daughter-of-Amundi, mother-of Stein, father-of Gudrun, mother-of Arnfrid who-was Digur-Helgi married-to.	Amundi also had a daughter named Rannveig, the mother of Stein, the father of Gudrun, the mother of Arnfrid, who was married to Stout-Helgi.
Þorkatla var og Ámundadóttir, móðir Arnbjargar, móður Finns prests og Þorgeirs og Þuríðar.	Thorkatla was also Daughter-of-Amundi, mother-of Arnbjorg, mother-of Fin the-priest and Thorgeir and Thorid.	Thorkatla was also a daughter of Amundi, the mother of Arnbjorg, the mother of Fin the priest, and Thorgeir and Thurid.
Og hefir margt höfðingsmanna frá þeim komið.	And have many prestigious-people from them coming.	And there were many prestigious people descended from them.
Og lýkur þar að segja frá Þorsteini stangarhögg.	And ends there to say from Thorstein Staff-Struck	And there ends the saga of Thorstein Staff-Struck.

Word List *(Old Icelandic to English)*

Old Icelandic	English

A, a

að	at, in, it, than, that, the, to, to-be, was, which
aðrir	other
af	of, of, off
afbragðsmaður	excellent-man, outstanding-man
aftan	evening
alla	all
allan	all
allra	all, all
allt	all, all
allur	all
alvöru	seriously
andaðist	died
annar	another, one
annarra	other
annarrar	of-the-other
annarri	another
annars	another's
armastur	miserable
Arnbjargar	Arnbjorg (name)
Arnfríðar	Arnfrid (name)
atburð	accident
atburði	events
augað	eye

Á, á

á	a, about, at, in, of, on, the, to
áður	before
Ámunda	Amundi's (name), Amundi's (name)
Ámundadóttir	Daughter-of-Amundi (name)
Ámundi	Amundi (name)
átt	had
átti	had, married, married-to
áttu	had

Æ, æ

æptu	called-out
æsku	youth
ætla	suppose
ætlar	suppose
ætluðu	intended
ætlum	suppose
ævi	life

B, b

bað	asked
báða	both
bæði	both
bæta	compensation
bæturnar	compensation
bak	back
banahögg	death-blow
bar	carried
barist	carried
barst	overcome
bauð	invited
beiðast	ask
bekk	bench
berjast	fight, fighting, fought
berst	fight
betra	better
betur	better
bíða	abide
biður	asked
bind	tie
bindur	bound, tied
biskups	the-bishop
bítast	bite
bítur	bite
Bjarna	Bjarni (name), Bjarni's (name)
Bjarni	Bjarni (name)

Word List (Old Icelandic to English)

Old Icelandic	English
bjó	lived
bjóða	to-invite
björg	help
blinda	the-blind
Böðvarsdal	Bodvarsdale (name)
Böðvarsdóttur	Daughter-of-Bodvar (name)
bograð	stoop
bolinn	torso
borð	the-table
borða	the-tables
borði	the-table
Borg	Borg (place)
bræður	brothers
bregð	move
brugðust	broke
brúnina	eyebrow
búi	estate
búið	prepared
búst	settle
býr	prepared

D, d

Old Icelandic	English
dældarmaður	gentle-man
dæma	deemed
dæmi	judging
dag	day, the-day
daga	day
dagmálum	mid-morning
dauðadags	death-day
Digur-Helgi	Digur-Helgi (name)
dilkahöfuð	sheep-heads
dóttir	daughter
dóttur	daughter
draga	drag
drekk	drink
drengskap	honour
drepið	killed
durum	doorway

E, e

Old Icelandic	English
eða	or
ef	if
eftir	after
eg	I, I-am
eggja	encouraging
eiga	have, only, own
eigi	alone, none, not, not-be
eina	one
Einars	Einar (name)
einn	alone, one
einskis	nothing, only
einvígis	single-combat
eitt	one, one-thing
ekki	not
eldahússveggnum	fire-house-wall
eldri	older
elli	age
em	am
en	about, and, as, but, still, than, that, then, when
engan	none
engi	no-one, nothing
engir	none
engu	none
enn	still, then
er	are, as, at, but, is, is-it, of, than, that, was, what, when, where, which, who, who-are, who-was, with
erfiðinu	difficulty
erindlaust	errand-lost
ert	are
ertu	are-you
eru	are, are-you, they-were
erum	are, they-are

Word List (Old Icelandic to English)

Old Icelandic	English

F, f

fá	few, get, give, had
faðir	father, father-of
færa	bring, travelled
færi	brought, went
færir	brought
fann	found
far	go, Travel
fara	going, to-go, travel, travelled, went
farið	going, gone
farinn	gone
fastlegra	fixed
feðgar	father-and-son
feginn	joyful
fékk	got
félítill	fee-little
féll	fell
fer	travel, travelled, went
ferð	journey
finni	find
Finns	Fin (name)
finnum	finding
fjár	fee
fjölmenni	followers
fjölmennur	followers
fjörsins	life
fleira	more
flekk	stain
föður	father, father-of
fór	travelled
för	for
forlagðir	mislaid
forverk	for-work
forverks	working
fótum	feet
frá	from
frændi	kinsmen
frændum	kinsmen
framfærslumenn	paupers
frekt	eagerly
frekur	eager
fretkarla	contemptible-man
fróa	console
frýjuorð	taunting
fullgoldið	fully-golded
fylgdi	followed
fyrir	before, for
fyrnast	age
fyrra	before

G, g

gæfa	gift
gætti	guarded
gakk	come, go
gamall	old
ganga	go, going, went
gangi	go
garð	fences
garðinn	meadow
gegnum	through
gekk	went
geldingahöfuð	ram-heads
gengi	went
gengu	went
gengur	went
gera	do
gerði	did
gerðist	became
gerðu	do-you
gerir	make
gerr	do
gert	done
Gissurarson	Gizurarson (name)
gjarna	gladly
glæp	the-wicked
goða	the-chieftain
gráta	weeping
Guðmundar	Gudmund's (name)
Guðnýjar	Gudny (name)
Guðríðar	Gudrid (name)
Guðrún	Gudrun (name)
Guðrúnar	Gudrun (name)

Word List (Old Icelandic to English)

Old Icelandic	English	Old Icelandic	English

H, h

Old Icelandic	English
hætta	conclude, concluded, risk
hafa	had, have
hafði	had
hafi	had, has, have
haft	had
halds	hold
Halla	Halla (name)
Hallfríður	Hallfrid (name)
hallkvæmara	hold-fulfil
háls	neck
hana	her
handsöl	pledge
hann	he, him, it
hans	him, his
happi	luck
harðfengi	toughness
harmar	harm
haustið	autumn
hefi	have
hefir	had, has, have
hefna	revenge
heill	healthy
heim	home
heima	home
heiman	home
heimskur	stupid
heimti	claim
heit	promises
heitir	named
heitum	called
heldur	rather
Helgu	Helga (name)
heljarmannsins	cursed-man-this
helst	rather
hélt	held
hendi	arms
hendinni	his-hand
hendir	happens
hendur	hands
hér	here
héraði	the-district
héraðinu	the-district
hest	the-horse
hesta	horses
hestaats	horse-fight
hestahúsinu	horse-house
hestana	horses
hestarnir	the-horses
hestastafnum	horse-staffs
hestasvein	horse-boy
hestaþingi	horse-fight
hestaþinginu	horse-fight
hesti	horse
hestinum	horses
hestum	horses
hestur	horse
hesturinn	horse
hét	named, was-named
hey	hay
heyrðu	heard
hið	then
hingað	here, there
hinn	the
hitta	met
hitti	met
hittir	found
hjá	beside
hjó	struck
hjóstu	have-you-hit
hjuggust	hewed
hleypur	ran
hlífar	protection
hlífarlaus	helpless
hljóp	ran
hlut	lot
hluta	part
hlýða	listen
hlýddi	followed
höfði	head
höfðingja	chieftains
höfðingsmanna	prestigious-people
höfðu	had
Hofi	Hof (place)
hofs	Hof, Hof (place)
höfuð	head
höfuðbeinunum	head-bone
högg	a-strike, been-struck, blow, striking

Word List (Old Icelandic to English)

Old Icelandic	English
höggum	blows
höggunum	the-blows
höggur	struck
höggva	strike
höggvið	the-blow
hól	hill
hólinn	hill, the-hill
hönd	hand
honum	he, him, his
hræddur	scared
hreysti	valour
hrósið	praise
hrossa	horses, the-horses
hrossahúss	horse-house
hrossahússins	horse-house
hrossamaður	horse-man
hrossin	horses
hug	spirit, thoughts
hugði	thought
hún	her, it, she
hundur	a-dog
húskarl	servant
húskarla	servants
húskarlar	servants
húss	house
hvað	that, what
hvar	where
hvarf	disappeared
hvatti	sharpened
hvenær	when
hver	any, each, who, why
hvernig	how
hversu	how-many
hvert	what, where
hví	Why
hvílir	rested
hvoftana	mouths
hvorn	each
hvort	whether
hvortveggi	each
hvorumtveggja	each-other

I, i

Old Icelandic	English
illt	ill
inn	in, inside
innar	in

Í, í

í	at, I, in, into, on, this, to

J, j

jafnhátt	equally
jarða	buried
jarðaður	earthed
Jól	Yule (name)

K, k

kalla	call
kallaður	called
kallsi	taunted
kann	know
kappi	warrior, warriors
karl	old-man, the-old-man
karli	the-old-man
kaup	purchase
kemur	came, comes
kenna	be-known
kenni	know
kippti	dragged
kné	knees
Kolbeinn	Kolbein (name)
kölluðu	called
kom	came
koma	came
komið	coming
kominn	came, come, coming
komnir	coming
komu	came
kona	the-woman

Word List (Old Icelandic to English)

Old Icelandic	English
konan	the-woman
konu	woman
konum	women
konur	women
köstuðust	exchanged
kvað	said
kvenna	women
kynlegt	surprised, wonder
kynsæll	kin-blessed
kyrrt	peace, still

L, l

Old Icelandic	English
lá	lay
lægi	laying
lækjarins	stream
lætur	behaved, had, has
lagði	had, laid
lagðir	had
lagðist	laid
lambahöfuðin	lambs-heads
láta	had
laus	loose
leggja	to-lay
leið	pass
leik	sport
leit	looked
leita	look-for, looking-for
lengi	along, long
lengur	longer
lét	had
letja	discourage
leyfa	allow
leyni	keep-secret
líður	passed
lifir	alive, live
líklegastir	likeliest
líklegt	likely
lítið	little
litlu	little
lofa	promise
lögsögumaður	lawspeaker
lokhvílu	bed-closet
lostinn	struck
lukka	luck

Old Icelandic	English
lýkur	ends
lýstur	struck
lýtur	stooped

M, m

Old Icelandic	English
má	may
maður	a-man, man, the-man
maðurinn	the-man
mæl	say
mæla	speak
mælast	speak
mælir	speak
mælt	spoken
mælti	said, spoke
mæltu	spoke-of
mætti	may, might
Magnús	Magnus (name)
Magnúss	Magnus (name)
maki	matched
maklegleika	serve-you-right
mál	a-case
mánaðarfró	a-month-from
mann	man
manna	men, people's
manni	man
manninn	people
manns	man
marga	many
margir	many
margt	many
með	between, with
meðan	as-long-as
mega	may-be
meir	more
meira	more
menn	men, people
mér	for-me, I, me, myself, to-me
mesti	most
meta	meet
mig	me, to-me
mikið	much
mikil	great
mikill	great, much

Word List (Old Icelandic to English)

Old Icelandic	English
miklir	much
miklu	much
mín	me, mine
mína	mine
minn	me, mine
minnar	my
minni	mine
mínum	mine, my
mislagðar	misplaced
missa	miss
mjög	much
móðir	mother, mother-of
móður	mother-of
mörgum	many
morgun	morning
morguninn	morning
móti	towards
mun	shall, should, will, would
mundi	could, thought, would
mundir	would
mundu	would
mundum	would
muni	shall, would
munt	shall, would
muntu	shall-you, you-should

N, n

Old Icelandic	English
nær	near
naut	a-bull, bull
né	nor
nefndur	named
nenni	bothers, care
nennti	wanted
niður	down, downed
nokkuð	any-at-all
nokkura	some
nokkuru	somewhat
nokkurum	some
nóttina	the-night
nú	now

O, o

Old Icelandic	English
ofan	across, down, over
ofmælt	or-speaking, said-too-much
oft	often
oftar	often
og	also, and
okkur	us
orða	words
orðið	worded, words
orðum	words
Orms	Orm (name)
oss	us, we

Ó, ó

Old Icelandic	English
ógæfa	misfortune
ógifta	un-gift
óhapp	mishap
óhefnt	without-revenge
ójafnaðarmaður	un-equal-man
ómegð	without
ómerkir	unremarkable
ósæmd	dishonour
óvanari	not-used-to

Ö, ö

Old Icelandic	English
öðru	another
öðrum	others, the-other
öflugur	powerful
öllu	all
öndvegi	foremost-seat
öttu	matched
öxina	axe

P, p

Old Icelandic	English
prests	the-priest

Word List (Old Icelandic to English)

Old Icelandic	English

R, r

Old Icelandic	English
ráða	decide
ræða	discussing
ragan	cowardly
rann	ran
Rannveig	Rannveig (name)
rauðavíkingur	fierce-viking
reið	ride
reiðhesta	riding-horses
reis	rose
rekkjugólfið	bed-closet
ríða	to-ride
ríkara	more-powerful, stronger
ríkismanns	noble-man's
risti	carved
risu	rose
Rómaborg	Rome-city (place)
runnið	slipped

S, s

Old Icelandic	English
sá	saw, so
sæng	bed
sæti	sat
sagði	said, said, told, told
sagt	told
sakar	sake
saklausa	without-cause
sama	the-same
saman	together
samhéraðs	same-district
sárunum	injury
sat	sat
satt	TRUE
sátu	sat
sax	short-sword
saxi	short-sword
saxinu	short-sword
sé	is, see
seg	tell
segi	say
segir	said, say
segja	say, tell
seint	weak
sekan	guilty
seldu	sold
sem	as, as-if, which
sendi	sent
sér	himself, themselves, to-you
síðan	afterwards, then
síðar	afterwards
síðasta	last
Síðu-Hallsson	Sidu-Hallson (name)
Sighvats	Sighvat (name)
Sigríði	Sigrid (name)
sín	him, his
sína	his, theirs
sinn	his, that
sinnar	his
sinni	his
síns	hers, his
sínu	his
sínum	his, their, with-his
sitja	settle
sitji	situated
sitt	yours
sjálfbjargi	self-supported
sjálfur	himself, myself
sjónlausum	sight-less
sjónlítill	seeing-little
skal	shall
skalt	shall
skaltu	shall, shall-you
skammt	short
skap	mood
skapi	mind
Skegg-Broddi	Skegg-Broddi (name)
skelfur	shaking
skilið	divided
skip	ship
skipta	exchange
skjöld	shield
skjöldinn	shield
skjöldu	shields
skjöldur	shield
skógarmaður	outlaw
skógarmaðurinn	outlawed

Word List (Old Icelandic to English)

Old Icelandic	English
skoltinn	jaw
skörulegast	noble
skóþvengur	shoe-thongs
skyldi	should, should-be
skyldu	should
skyrtublaði	shirt-sheet
skyrtum	shirts
slíka	such
slíkt	such
slíkum	such
slíta	wear-out
sljóvgast	blunt
smærra	a-smaller
snarlegra	speedily
snemma	early
Snorra	Snorri (name)
sofa	slept
sögðu	told
sögðust	said
sögur	the-sagas
sökum	sake
son	a-son, son
sonar	son, son's
sonardauðinn	son-death
sonur	son
spara	spare
spurði	asked
stað	place
stakk	pushed
standa	stand
stangað	gored
Stangarhögg	Staff-Struck (name)
sté	stepped
Steins	Stein (name)
stendur	standing
stilltur	composed, orderly
stóð	stood
stoða	stand
stoðar	avail, support
stóðhross	stud-horses
stórt	great
stundar	awhile's
stundu	time
Sturlusona	the-Sturlusons (name)
sú	that
suður	south
sumar	summer
Sunnudal	Sunnudal (place)
svaraði	answered
svarar	answered
svefns	sleep
sverð	sword
sverðið	the-sword
svíða	singe
svíðið	singe
sviðuelda	bonfires
svíkja	betray
svíma	dizziness
Svínfellings	Svinafellings (name)
svo	so
svöruðu	answered
syni	son
sýnist	seems
sýta	mourn

T, t

Old Icelandic	English
tak	take
taka	take, takes, took
talað	talking, told
tali	talking
tals	talk
taumana	reins
tekur	takes, took
tíðast	news
tíðinda	news
til	there, to, towards, until
tilræði	assault
títt	reported
togað	pulled
tók	took
tókum	taking
tröll	trolls
trúmaður	true-man
trúr	TRUE
trútt	truth
tungu	tongue
tungunni	tongue
túni	field

Word List (Old Icelandic to English)

Old Icelandic	English
tvo	two

Þ, þ

Old Icelandic	English
þá	then
það	it, that, this
þaðan	from
þær	there
þagað	silence
þar	there
þau	then, they
þegar	straightaway, when
þeim	their, them, those
þeir	they
þeirra	their, they, those
þeirri	their, there
þenna	this
þér	of-you, to-you, you, your
þess	this
þessa	this
þessi	this
þessu	this
þessum	this
þetta	that, this
þið	you, you-two
þig	you
þín	you, yours
þína	yours
þingmönnum	assembly-men
þinn	yours
þíns	yours
þínu	you
þínum	you, yours
þó	though
þoli	tolerate
Þórarinn	Thorarin (name)
Þórarni	Thorarin (name)
Þórð	Thord (name)
Þórðar	Thord (name), Thord's (name)
Þórdísar	Thordis (name)
Þórður	Thord (name)
Þorgeirs	Thorgeir (name)
Þorgríms	Thorgrim's (name)
Þórhall	Thorhall (name)
Þórhallur	Thorhall (name)
Þorkatla	Thorkatla (name)
Þorstein	Thorstein (name)
Þorsteini	Thorstein (name), Thorstein's (name)
Þorsteinn	Thorstein (name)
Þorsteins	Thorstein (name), Thorstein's (name)
Þóru	Thora (name)
Þorvald	Thorvald (name)
Þorvaldur	Thorvald (name)
þótt	though
þótti	thought
þræla	thralls
þraut	struggle
þrautbestur	persistent
þrek	strength
þriggja	three
þrjá	three
þú	you
þuklaði	felt
þungt	difficulty
þurfa	need
Þuríðar	Thorid (name)
því	accordingly, because, since, therefore, which
þykir	consider, seem, seemed, seems, think
þykja	think, to-think
þykjast	consider, thought
þyrstir	thirsty

U, u

Old Icelandic	English
um	about
una	content
undan	away, away-from, from-under
undir	submit, under, up-to
ungum	young
uns	until
upp	got-up, up
uppaustrarmenn	gossipers
utan	out, out-travel

Word List (Old Icelandic to English)

Old Icelandic	English

Ú, ú

úr	from, out-of
út	out, outside
úti	out, outside

V, v

vægt	mercy
vænt	expect
væri	was, would
vaknar	awoke
vakti	awoke
valdi	will
vanheilsu	failing-health
vann	worked
vant	difficulty, want
var	was, were
vara	would-be
varð	became, was
varði	expected
varðist	defended
varðveitti	looked-after
varlega	warily
varnaði	warn
varstu	were-you
Vateri	Sutri (place)
vegið	killed
veginn	killed
veit	know
veita	to-give
veitti	granted
vekja	wake
vel	well
ver	be
vér	we, we-are
vera	be, had-been
verða	be, become, comes
verður	become, worth
verið	been
verk	work
verks	work
verr	worse, worst
verra	worse
veturinn	winter
við	against, in, with
víða	widely
víg	killing
Víga-Bjarna	Killer-Bjarni (name)
vígið	the-killing
vígkænn	battle-cunning
vil	wish
vildi	will, willed, wish, would
vilja	will, wish
viljið	wish
vill	will
vilt	will, wish
vinna	win
vinsælli	popular
virðing	worthy
virðingu	honour, worthiness
virðir	valued
vísar	refer, saw
vist	hospitality, provisions
víst	certain, knew
vísu	certain
vita	know, known
víti	penalty
vits	wits
vitum	know
voðaverk	accident, an-accident
von	expect
vopn	weapon, weapons
vopna	weapons
vopnaskipti	weapons-exchange
vopnið	weapon
vorir	our
voru	were

Y, y

yður	of-you
yfir	over
ykkur	you
Yngvildar	Yngvild's (name)
Yngvildur	Yngvild (name)

Word List *(English to Old Icelandic)*

English	Old Icelandic
A, a	
a	á
about	á, á, á
at	á, á, að, að
all	alla, allan, allra, allra, allt, allt, allur, Ámunda
Amundi's (name)	Ámunda, Ámunda
Amundi (name)	Ámundi
another	annar, annarri, annars
another's	annars
Arnbjorg (name)	Arnbjargar
Arnfrid (name)	Arnfríðar
accident	atburð, atburði
asked	bað, báða, bæði
ask	beiðast
abide	bíða
after	eftir
alone	eigi, Einars
age	elli, em
am	em
and	en, en
as	en, en, er
are	er, er, er, er
are-you	ertu, eru
autumn	haustið
arms	hendi
a-strike	högg
a-dog	hundur
any	hver
along	lengi
allow	leyfa
alive	lifir
a-man	maður
a-case	mál
a-month-from	mánaðarfró
as-long-as	meðan
a-bull	naut
any-at-all	nokkuð
across	ofan
also	og
axe	öxina

English	Old Icelandic
as-if	sem
afterwards	síðan, síðar
a-smaller	smærra
a-son	son
avail	stoðar
awhile's	stundar
answered	svaraði, svarar, sviðuelda
assembly-men	þingmönnum
accordingly	því
assault	tilræði
away	undan
away-from	undan
awoke	vaknar, vakti
against	við
an-accident	voðaverk
B, b	
before	áður, æptu, ætluðu
both	báða, bæði
back	bak
bench	bekk
better	betra, betur
bound	bindur
bite	bítast, bítur
Bjarni (name)	Bjarna, Bjarna
Bjarni's (name)	Bjarna
Bodvarsdale (name)	Böðvarsdal
Borg (place)	Borg
brothers	bræður
broke	brugðust
but	en, er
bring	færa
brought	færi, færir
became	gerðist, gerðu
beside	hjá
been-struck	högg
blow	högg
blows	höggum
buried	jarða
be-known	kenna

Word List (English to Old Icelandic)

English	*Old Icelandic*
behaved	lætur
bed-closet	lokhvílu, lukka
between	með
bull	naut
bothers	nenni
bed	sæng
blunt	sljóvgast
bonfires	sviðuelda
betray	svíkja
because	því
be	ver, vera, vera
become	verða, verða
been	verið
battle-cunning	vígkænn

C, c

English	*Old Icelandic*
called-out	æptu
compensation	bæta, bæturnar
carried	bar, barist
contemptible-man	fretkarla
console	fróa
come	gakk, gakk
conclude	hætta
concluded	hætta
claim	heimti
called	heitum, Helgu, heljarmannsins
cursed-man-this	heljarmannsins
chieftains	höfðingja
call	kalla
came	kemur, kemur, kenna, kenni, kippti
comes	kemur, kenna
coming	komið, kominn, kominn
could	mundi
care	nenni
cowardly	ragan
carved	risti
composed	stilltur
consider	þykir, þykjast
content	una
certain	víst, víst

D, d

English	*Old Icelandic*
Daughter-of-Amundi (name)	Ámundadóttir
died	andaðist
death-blow	banahögg
Daughter-of-Bodvar (name)	Böðvarsdóttur
deemed	dæma
day	dag, daga
death-day	dauðadags
Digur-Helgi (name)	Digur-Helgi
daughter	dóttir, dóttur
drag	draga
drink	drekk
doorway	durum
difficulty	erfiðinu, erindlaust, ert
do	gera, gerði
did	gerði
do-you	gerðu
done	gert
disappeared	hvarf
dragged	kippti
discourage	letja
down	niður, niður
downed	niður
dishonour	ósæmd
decide	ráða
discussing	ræða
divided	skilið
dizziness	svíma
defended	varðist

E, e

English	*Old Icelandic*
excellent-man	afbragðsmaður
evening	aftan
events	atburði
eye	augað
eyebrow	brúnina
estate	búi
encouraging	eggja
Einar (name)	Einars

Word List (English to Old Icelandic)

English	Old Icelandic
errand-lost	erindlaust
eagerly	frekt
eager	frekur
each	hver, hvernig, hversu
each-other	hvorumtveggja
equally	jafnhátt
earthed	jarðaður
exchanged	köstuðust
ends	lýkur
exchange	skipta
early	snemma
expect	vænt, vaknar
expected	varði

F, f

English	Old Icelandic
fight	berjast, berjast
fighting	berjast
fought	berjast
fire-house-wall	eldahússveggnum
few	fá
father	faðir, faðir
father-of	faðir, færa
found	fann, far
fixed	fastlegra
father-and-son	feðgar
fee-little	félítill
fell	féll
find	finni
Fin (name)	Finns
finding	finnum
fee	fjár
followers	fjölmenni, fjölmennur
for	för, forlagðir
for-work	forverk
feet	fótum
from	frá, frændi, frændum
fully-golded	fullgoldið
followed	fylgdi, fyrir
fences	garð
for-me	mér
foremost-seat	öndvegi
fierce-viking	rauðavíkingur
felt	þuklaði
field	túni
from-under	undan
failing-health	vanheilsu

G, g

English	Old Icelandic
gentle-man	dældarmaður
get	fá
give	fá
go	far, fara, farið, farið
going	fara, farið, farið
gone	farið, farinn
got	fékk
gift	gæfa
guarded	gætti
Gizurarson (name)	Gissurarson
gladly	gjarna
Gudmund's (name)	Guðmundar
Gudny (name)	Guðnýjar
Gudrid (name)	Guðríðar
Gudrun (name)	Guðrún, Guðrúnar
great	mikil, mikill, mikill
guilty	sekan
gored	stangað
got-up	upp
gossipers	uppaustrarmenn
granted	veitti

H, h

English	Old Icelandic
had	átt, átti, átti, átti, áttu, augað, bað, báða, bæði, bæta, bæturnar, bak, banahögg, bar, barist
help	björg
honour	drengskap, drepið
have	eiga, eigi, Einars, einn, eldahússveggnum
has	hafi, hafi, haft
hold	halds
Halla (name)	Halla
Hallfrid (name)	Hallfríður
hold-fulfil	hallkvæmara
her	hana, hann

Word List (English to Old Icelandic)

English	Old Icelandic	English	Old Icelandic
he	hann, hann		
him	hann, hann, hans, hans	**I, i**	
his	hans, happi, harmar, haustið, hefi, hefir, hefir, hefir, heill, heim	in	á, að, að, að, áður, æptu
		it	að, áður, æptu, ætluðu
harm	harmar	intended	ætluðu
healthy	heill	invited	bauð
home	heim, heima, heiman	if	ef
Helga (name)	Helgu	I	eg, eg, eggja
held	hélt	I-am	eg
his-hand	hendinni	is	er, er
happens	hendir	is-it	er
hands	hendur	into	í
here	hér, hesta	ill	illt
horses	hesta, hestaats, hestahúsinu, hestana, hestastafnum, hestasvein	inside	inn
		injury	sárunum
horse-fight	hestaats, hestahúsinu, hestana	**J, j**	
horse-house	hestahúsinu, hestana, hestastafnum	judging	dæmi
horse-staffs	hestastafnum	joyful	feginn
horse-boy	hestasvein	journey	ferð
horse	hesti, hestinum, hestum	jaw	skoltinn
hay	hey	**K, k**	
heard	heyrðu		
have-you-hit	hjóstu		
hewed	hjuggust	killed	drepið, durum, ef
helpless	hlífarlaus	kinsmen	frændi, frændum
head	höfði, höfðingja	know	kann, kemur, kemur, kenna, kenni
Hof (place)	Hofi, hofs	knees	kné
Hof	hofs	Kolbein (name)	Kolbeinn
head-bone	höfuðbeinunum	kin-blessed	kynsæll
hill	hól, hólinn	keep-secret	leyni
hand	hönd	killing	víg
horse-man	hrossamaður	Killer-Bjarni (name)	Víga-Bjarna
house	húss	knew	víst
how	hvernig	known	vita
how-many	hversu		
himself	sér, síðan		
hers	síns		
had-been	vera		
hospitality	vist		

Word List (English to Old Icelandic)

English	*Old Icelandic*	*English*	*Old Icelandic*
		men	manna, manni
		many	marga, margir, margt, með

L, l

English	Old Icelandic
life	ævi, afbragðsmaður
lived	bjó
luck	happi, harmar
lot	hlut
listen	hlýða
lay	lá
laying	lægi
laid	lagði, lagðir
lambs-heads	lambahöfuðin
loose	laus
looked	leit
look-for	leita
looking-for	leita
long	lengi
longer	lengur
live	lifir
likeliest	líklegastir
likely	líklegt
little	lítið, litlu
lawspeaker	lögsögumaður
last	síðasta
looked-after	varðveitti

M, m

English	Old Icelandic
miserable	armastur
married	átti
married-to	átti
move	bregð
mid-morning	dagmálum
more	fleira, föður, föður
mislaid	forlagðir
meadow	garðinn
make	gerir
met	hitta, hitti
mouths	hvoftana
may	má, maður
man	maður, mætti, mætti, Magnús
might	mætti
Magnus (name)	Magnús, Magnúss
matched	maki, mál

English	Old Icelandic
men	manna, manni
many	marga, margir, margt, með
may-be	mega
me	mér, mér, mesti, meta
myself	mér, mesti
most	mesti
meet	meta
much	mikið, mikil, mikill, mikill, miklir
mine	mín, mína, minn, minn, minnar
my	minnar, minni
misplaced	mislagðar
miss	missa
mother	móðir
mother-of	móðir, móður
morning	morgun, morguninn
misfortune	ógæfa
mishap	óhapp
more-powerful	ríkara
mood	skap
mind	skapi
mourn	sýta
mercy	vægt

N, n

English	Old Icelandic
none	eigi, eigi, eigi, eina
not	eigi, eigi
not-be	eigi
nothing	einskis, einskis
no-one	engi
neck	háls
named	heitir, heldur, helst
near	nær
nor	né
now	nú
not-used-to	óvanari
noble-man's	ríkismanns
noble	skörulegast
need	þurfa
news	tíðast, tíðinda

Word List (English to Old Icelandic)

English	Old Icelandic	English	Old Icelandic
		peace	kyrrt
O, o		pass	leið
		passed	líður
of	á, á, á, á	promise	lofa
on	á, á	people's	manna
other	aðrir, æsku	people	manninn, með
off	af	powerful	öflugur
outstanding-man	afbragðsmaður	place	stað
one	annar, annarra, annarrar, barst	pushed	stakk
		persistent	þrautbestur
of-the-other	annarrar	pulled	togað
overcome	barst	popular	vinsælli
or	eða	provisions	vist
only	eiga, eiga	penalty	víti
own	eiga		
one-thing	eitt	**R, r**	
older	eldri		
old	gamall	ram-heads	geldingahöfuð
old-man	karl	risk	hætta
others	öðrum	revenge	hefna
over	ofan, öflugur	rather	heldur, helst
or-speaking	ofmælt	ran	hleypur, hlífar, hljóp
often	oft, oftar	rested	hvílir
Orm (name)	Orms	Rannveig (name)	Rannveig
outlaw	skógarmaður	ride	reið
outlawed	skógarmaðurinn	riding-horses	reiðhesta
orderly	stilltur	rose	reis, ríða
of-you	þér, þér	Rome-city (place)	Rómaborg
out-of	úr	reins	taumana
out	út, út, utan	reported	títt
outside	út, utan	refer	vísar
out-travel	utan		
our	vorir	**S, s**	
		suppose	ætla, ætlar, ætlum
P, p		seriously	alvöru
		stoop	bograð
prepared	búið, búst	settle	búst, býr
paupers	framfærslumenn	sheep-heads	dilkahöfuð
pledge	handsöl	single-combat	einvígis
promises	heit	still	en, en, en
protection	hlífar	stain	flekk
part	hluta	stupid	heimskur
prestigious-people	höfðingsmanna		
praise	hrósið		
purchase	kaup		

Word List (English to Old Icelandic)

English	*Old Icelandic*
struck	hjó, hleypur, hlífar, hljóp
striking	högg
strike	höggva
scared	hræddur
spirit	hug
she	hún
servant	húskarl
servants	húskarla, húskarlar
sharpened	hvatti
said	kvað, kvenna, kynlegt, kynlegt, kyrrt, kyrrt
surprised	kynlegt
stream	lækjarins
sport	leik
stooped	lýtur
say	mæl, mæla, mælast, mælir
speak	mæla, mælast, mælir
spoken	mælt
spoke	mælti
spoke-of	mæltu
serve-you-right	maklegleika
shall	mun, mun, mun, mun, mundi, mundi
should	mun, mun, mun
shall-you	muntu, muntu
some	nokkura, nokkuru
somewhat	nokkuru
said-too-much	ofmælt
stronger	ríkara
slipped	runnið
saw	sá, sá
so	sá, sæti
sat	sæti, sagði, sagði
sake	sakar, saklausa
same-district	samhéraðs
short-sword	sax, saxi, saxinu
see	sé
sold	seldu
sent	sendi
Sidu-Hallson (name)	Síðu-Hallsson
Sighvat (name)	Sighvats
Sigrid (name)	Sigríði
situated	sitji
self-supported	sjálfbjargi
sight-less	sjónlausum
seeing-little	sjónlítill
short	skammt
Skegg-Broddi (name)	Skegg-Broddi
shaking	skelfur
ship	skip
shield	skjöld, skjöldinn, skjöldu
shields	skjöldu
shoe-thongs	skóþvengur
should-be	skyldi
shirt-sheet	skyrtublaði
shirts	skyrtum
such	slíka, slíkt, slíkum
speedily	snarlegra
Snorri (name)	Snorra
slept	sofa
son	son, sonar, sonar, sonardauðinn
son's	sonar
son-death	sonardauðinn
spare	spara
stand	standa, Stangarhögg
Staff-Struck (name)	Stangarhögg
stepped	sté
Stein (name)	Steins
standing	stendur
stood	stóð
support	stoðar
stud-horses	stóðhross
south	suður
summer	sumar
Sunnudal (place)	Sunnudal
sleep	svefns
sword	sverð
singe	svíða, svíðið
Svinafellings (name)	Svínfellings
seems	sýnist, tak
silence	þagað
straightaway	þegar
struggle	þraut
strength	þrek
since	því
seem	þykir
seemed	þykir

82

Word List (English to Old Icelandic)

English	Old Icelandic	English	Old Icelandic
submit	undir	the-old-man	karl, karli
Sutri (place)	Vateri	the-woman	kona, konan
		to-lay	leggja
		the-man	maður, maðurinn
		to-me	mér, mig

T, t

English	Old Icelandic	English	Old Icelandic
		towards	móti, mun
the	á, á, að	the-night	nóttina
to	á, að, að, að	the-other	öðrum
than	að, að, að	the-priest	prests
that	að, að, að, að, að, að, aðrir, æsku	to-ride	ríða
		told	sagði, sagði, sagt, sakar, saklausa
to-be	að		
tie	bind	the-same	sama
tied	bindur	together	saman
the-bishop	biskups	true	
to-invite	bjóða	tell	seg, segi
the-blind	blinda	themselves	sér
torso	bolinn	to-you	sér, síðan
the-table	borð, borða	theirs	sína
the-tables	borða	their	sínum, sínum, sitja, sitji
the-day	dag		
then	en, en, engan, engi, engi, engir	the-sagas	sögur
		time	stundu
they-were	eru	the-Sturlusons (name)	Sturlusona
they-are	erum		
travelled	færa, færi, far, fara	the-sword	sverðið
Travel	far, fara, fara	take	tak, taka
to-go	fara	takes	taka, taka
taunting	frýjuorð	took	taka, talað, talað
through	gegnum	talking	talað, talað
the-wicked	glæp	talk	tals
the-chieftain	goða	they	þau, þegar, þegar
toughness	harðfengi	them	þeim
the-district	héraði, héraðinu	those	þeim, þeir
the-horse	hest	though	þó, þoli
the-horses	hestarnir, hét	tolerate	þoli
there	hingað, hinn, hjó, hleypur, hlífar	Thorarin (name)	Þórarinn, Þórarni
		Thord (name)	Þórð, Þórðar, Þórðar
the-blows	höggunum	Thord's (name)	Þórðar
the-blow	höggvið	Thordis (name)	Þórdísar
the-hill	hólinn	Thorgeir (name)	Þorgeirs
thoughts	hug	Thorgrim's (name)	Þorgríms
thought	hugði, hún, húskarl, húskarla	Thorhall (name)	Þórhall, Þórhallur
		Thorkatla (name)	Þorkatla
this	í, í, Jól, kallsi, kappi, kappi, karl, karl, karli	Thorstein (name)	Þorstein, Þorsteini, Þorsteini, Þorsteinn
taunted	kallsi		

Word List (English to Old Icelandic)

English	Old Icelandic	English	Old Icelandic
Thorstein's (name)	Þorsteini, Þorsteinn	where	er, er, er
Thora (name)	Þóru	who	er, er
Thorvald (name)	Þorvald, Þorvaldur	who-are	er
thralls	þræla	who-was	er
three	þriggja, þrjá	with	er, eru, erum
Thorid (name)	Þuríðar	went	færi, far, fara, fara, fara, fara, fer, fer
therefore	því	working	forverks
think	þykir, þykja	weeping	gráta
to-think	þykja	was-named	hét
thirsty	þyrstir	why	hver, hvert
taking	tókum	whether	hvort
trolls	tröll	warrior	kappi
true-man	trúmaður	warriors	kappi
true		woman	konu
truth	trútt	women	konum, konur, kvað
tongue	tungu, tungunni	wonder	kynlegt
two	tvo	will	mun, mun, mundi, mundi, mundir, mundu
to-give	veita		
the-killing	vígið	would	mun, mundi, mundi, mundir, mundu, mundum, muni, muni, munt

U, u

English	Old Icelandic
un-gift	ógifta
un-equal-man	ójafnaðarmaður
us	okkur, ómegð
unremarkable	ómerkir
until	til, títt
under	undir
up-to	undir
up	upp

English	Old Icelandic
wanted	nennti
without-revenge	óhefnt
without	ómegð
words	orða, orðið, orðið
worded	orðið
we	oss, óvanari
without-cause	saklausa
weak	seint
with-his	sínum
wear-out	slíta
worked	vann
want	vant
were	var, vara
would-be	vara
warily	varlega
warn	varnaði
were-you	varstu
wake	vekja
well	vel
we-are	vér
worth	verður
work	verk, verks

V, v

English	Old Icelandic
valour	hreysti
valued	virðir

W, w

English	Old Icelandic
was	að, að, aðrir, æsku, ætla
which	að, aðrir, æsku, ætla
when	en, engan, engi, engi
what	er, er, er

Word List (English to Old Icelandic)

English	Old Icelandic
worse	verr, verr
worst	verr
winter	veturinn
widely	víða
wish	vil, vildi, vildi, vildi, vildi
willed	vildi
win	vinna
worthy	virðing
worthiness	virðingu
wits	vits
weapon	vopn, vopn
weapons	vopn, vopna
weapons-exchange	vopnaskipti

Y, y

English	Old Icelandic
youth	æsku
Yule (name)	Jól
you-should	muntu
yours	sitt, sjálfbjargi, sjónlausum, sjónlítill, skal, skalt
you	þér, þér, þess, þessa, þessi, þessu, þessum, þetta
your	þér
you-two	þið
young	ungum
Yngvild's (name)	Yngvildar
Yngvild (name)	Yngvildur

A Word Comparison of Old Norse and Old Icelandic Words

Old Norse	Old Icelandic	English	Old Norse	Old Icelandic	English
áðr	áður	before	einum	einn	one
æfi	ævi	life	einvigis	einvígis	single-combat
afbragðsmaðr	afbragðsmaður	outstanding-man	ek	eg	I
			ek	eg	I-am
allr	allur	all	ekki	eigi	not
annarr	annar	another	eldhúsveggnum	eldahússveggnum	fire-house-wall
annarr	annar	one			
armastr	armastur	miserable	ellri	eldri	older
at	að	at	engis	einskis	nothing
at	að	it	engis	einskis	only
at	að	than	enn	en	and
at	að	that	enn	en	as
at	að	to	enn	en	but
at	að	to-be	enn	en	than
at	til	to	enn	en	then
augat	augað	eye	enn	en	when
barizt	barist	carried	énn	en	but
bart	barst	overcome	er	em	am
batt	bindur	bound	er	ert	are
berjumst	berst	fight	er	sem	as
best	hest	the-horse	er	sem	which
betr	betur	better	er	þegar	when
biða	bíða	abide	erindislaust	erindlaust	errand-lost
biðr	biður	asked	ertú	ertu	are-you
bindr	bindur	tied	eru	erum	they-are
bítr	bítur	bite	farit	farið	going
bograt	bograð	stoop	farit	farið	gone
bræðr	bræður	brothers	fekk	fékk	got
búit	búið	prepared	félitill	félítill	fee-little
bústú	búst	settle	fell	féll	fell
dældarmaðr	dældarmaður	gentle-man	ferr	fer	travel
dauða-dags	dauðadags	death-day	ferr	fer	travelled
dilka-höfuð	dilkahöfuð	sheep-heads	finna	finni	find
dœmi	dæmi	judging	finnim	finnum	finding
drepit	drepið	killed	fjölmennr	fjölmennur	followers
dugi	hug	spirit	fóður	föður	father
eðr	eða	or	fœra	færa	bring
eigi	ekki	not	fœra	færa	travelled
eigu	eiga	only	fœri	færi	brought

A Word Comparison of Old Norse and Old Icelandic

Old Norse	Old Icelandic	English	Old Norse	Old Icelandic	English
fœri	færi	went	hlífarlauss	hlífarlaus	helpless
fœrir	færir	brought	hlut	hluta	part
fór	fer	went	höfuðbeinum	höfuðbeinunum	head-bone
forverka	forverks	working	höggr	höggur	struck
framfœrslumenn	framfærslumenn	paupers	hölinn	hólinn	the-hill
frekr	frekur	eager	höllinn	hólinn	the-hill
frýju-orð	frýjuorð	taunting	hon	hún	her
fullgoldit	fullgoldið	fully-golded	hon	hún	it
ganga	gangi	go	hon	hún	she
garðinu	garðinn	meadow	hræddr	hræddur	scared
geldinga-höfuð	geldingahöfuð	ram-heads	hrósit	hrósið	praise
gengr	gengur	went	hrossahúsi	hrossahúss	horse-house
gerðú	gerðu	do-you	hrossamaðr	hrossamaður	horse-man
gjarnan	gjarna	gladly	hugða	hugði	thought
glœp	glæp	the-wicked	hváftana	hvoftana	mouths
góða	goða	the-chieftain	hvárn	hvorn	each
gott	eitt	one	hvárrtveggja	hvortveggi	each
Guðríðr	Guðríðar	Gudrid (name)	hvárt	hvort	whether
hála	háls	neck	hvárumtveggja	hvorumtveggja	each-other
haldkvæmara	hallkvæmara	hold-fulfil	hvat	hvað	what
haustit	haustið	autumn	hverr	hver	any
höggunum	höggunum	the-blows	hverr	hver	each
heimskr	heimskur	stupid	hverr	hver	who
heimta	heimti	claim	hverr	hver	why
heldr	heldur	rather	hvi	hví	Why
helt	hélt	held	í	á	in
helzt	helst	rather	Ingveldr	Yngvildur	Yngvild (name)
hendr	hendur	hands	Ingveldra	Yngvildar	Yngvild's (name)
hendr	hönd	hand	inn	innar	in
heraðinu	héraði	the-district	jarðaðr	jarðaður	earthed
herjast	berjast	fighting	kals	kallsi	taunted
hesta-ats	hestaats	horse-fight	karls	karli	the-old-man
hesthúsinn	hestahúsinu	horse-house	kemr	kemur	came
hestr	hestur	horse	kemr	kemur	comes
hestr	hesturinn	horse	kenni	kann	know
hestunum	hestinum	horses	kipti	kippti	dragged
hiífar	hlífar	protection	koma	komu	came
hingat	hingað	here	komit	komið	coming
hingat	hingað	there	kváðust	sögðust	said
hit	hið	then	kyrt	kyrrt	peace
hleypr	hleypur	ran			

A Word Comparison of Old Norse and Old Icelandic

Old Norse	Old Icelandic	English	Old Norse	Old Icelandic	English
kyrt	kyrrt	still	mjök	mjög	much
lætr	lætur	behaved	munda	mundi	would
lætr	lætur	had	mundak	mundi	would
lætr	lætur	has	muni	mun	would
lágði	lagði	laid	muntú	muntu	shall-you
lausir	laus	loose	nefndr	nefndur	named
laust	lýstur	struck	nenta	nennti	wanted
lengr	lengi	along	niðr	niður	down
leyna	leyni	keep-secret	niðr	niður	downed
líðr	líður	passed	nökkura	nokkura	some
liflr	lifir	live	nökkuru	nokkuru	somewhat
liklegastir	líklegastir	likeliest	nökkurum	nokkurum	some
lítt	lítið	little	nökkut	nokkuð	any-at-all
loekjarins	lækjarins	stream	œptu	æptu	called-out
lögsögumaðr	lögsögumaður	lawspeaker	œsku	æsku	youth
			öflugr	öflugur	powerful
lýkr	lýkur	ends	Ögmundr	Ámundi	Amundi (name)
lýstr	lýstur	struck			
lýtr	lýtur	stooped	ójafnaðar	ójafnaðarmaður	un-equal-man
maðr	maður	a-man			
maðr	maður	man	ok	og	also
maðr	maður	the-man	ok	og	and
maðrinn	maðurinn	the-man	okkr	okkur	us
mælti	sagði	said	ómjúkir	ómerkir	unremarkable
mætta	mætti	may	öngu	engu	none
mætta	mætti	might	ór	úr	from
Magnus	Magnús	Magnus (name)	ör	úr	out-of
			orð	orða	words
Magnúsar	Magnúss	Magnus (name)	orðit	orðið	worded
			orðit	orðið	words
málit	mál	a-case	ósœmd	ósæmd	dishonour
man	mun	shall	reist	risti	carved
man	mun	should	rekkjugðlfit	rekkjugólfið	bed-closet
mánaðar-frá	mánaðarfró	a-month-from	rekkjugólfit	rekkjugólfið	bed-closet
mann	manninn	people	ríkar	ríkara	stronger
mant	munt	shall	rikara	ríkara	more-powerful
mant	munt	would			
megi	mega	may-be	rísa	risu	rose
meirr	meir	more	rœða	ræða	discussing
mik	mig	me	Rúmaborg	Rómaborg	Rome-city (place)
mik	mig	to-me			
mikit	mikið	much	runnit	runnið	slipped
min	mín	me	sagði	kvað	said
mínir	minn	mine	sakir	sakar	sake

A Word Comparison of Old Norse and Old Icelandic

Old Norse	Old Icelandic	English
samheraðs	samhéraðs	same-district
segi	segja	tell
segir	kvað	said
segir	sagði	said
segir	sagði	told
segja	sögðu	told
siðara	síðasta	last
Siðu-Hallsson	Síðu-Hallsson	Sidu-Hallson (name)
siti	sitji	situated
sjálfr	sjálfur	himself
sjálfr	sjálfur	myself
sjönlausum	sjónlausum	sight-less
sjónlitill	sjónlítill	seeing-little
skaltú	skaltu	shall
skaltú	skaltu	shall-you
skamt	skammt	short
skelfr	skelfur	shaking
skifta	skipta	exchange
skilit	skilið	divided
skjöldinn	skjöld	shield
skjöldr	skjöldur	shield
skógarmaðr	skógarmaður	outlaw
skógarmaðrinn	skógarmaðurinn	outlawed
skörugligast	skörulegast	noble
skóþvengir	skóþvengur	shoe-thongs
slæfast	sljóvgast	blunt
slika	slíka	such
slikum	slíkum	such
slita	slíta	wear-out
snarligra	snarlegra	speedily
sóknum	sökum	sake
son	sonur	son
sonardauðinn	sonardauðinn	son-death
sonr	sonur	son
spyrr	spurði	asked
Stangarhöggs	Stangarhögg	Staff-Struck (name)
stangat	stangað	gored
störmenna	höfðingsmanna	prestigious-people
stendr	stendur	standing
stilltr	stilltur	orderly
stiltr	stilltur	composed
suðr	suður	south
svá	svo	so
svarar	svaraði	answered
sverðit	sverðið	the-sword
sviðelda	sviðuelda	bonfires
sviðit	svíðið	singe
svivirðing	virðing	worthy
talat	talað	told
tekr	tekur	took
þagat	þagað	silence
þat	það	it
þat	það	that
þat	það	this
Þórarinn	Þórarinn	Thorarin (name)
Þórsteinn	Þorsteinn	Thorstein (name)
þefri	þeirri	there
þeira	þeirra	their
þeira	þeirra	they
þeira	þeirra	those
þeiri	þeirri	their
þeiri	þeirri	there
þér	þið	you-two
þessarra	þessa	this
þik	þig	you
þo	þó	though
Þórarins	Þórarni	Thorarin (name)
Þórðr	Þórður	Thord (name)
Þórgeirs	Þorgeirs	Thorgeir (name)
Þórgríms	Þorgríms	Thorgrim's (name)
Þórhallr	Þórhallur	Thorhall (name)
Þórkatla	Þorkatla	Thorkatla (name)
Þórn	Þóru	Thora (name)
Þórstein	Þorstein	Thorstein (name)
Þórsteini	Þorsteini	Thorstein (name)

A Word Comparison of Old Norse and Old Icelandic

Old Norse	Old Icelandic	English
Þórsteini	Þorsteini	Thorstein (name)
Þórsteini	Þorsteini	Thorstein's (name)
Þórsteinn	Þorsteinn	Thorstein (name)
Þórsteins	Þorsteini	Thorstein (name)
Þórsteins	Þorsteins	Thorstein (name)
Þórsteins	Þorsteins	Thorstein's (name)
Þórvald	Þorvald	Thorvald (name)
Þórvaldr	Þorvaldur	Thorvald (name)
þrautbeztr	þrautbestur	persistent
Þuriðar	Þuríðar	Thorid (name)
þykki	þykir	consider
þykki	þykir	seems
þykki	þykir	think
þykkir	þykir	seem
þykkir	þykir	seemed
þykkir	þykir	seems
þykkir	þykir	think
þykkja	þykja	to-think
þykkjast	þykjast	consider
þykkjast	þykjast	thought
tíl	til	to
togat	togað	pulled
troll	tröll	trolls
trú-maðr	trúmaður	true-man
tuni	túni	field
tvá	tvo	two
unz	uns	until
útan	utan	out
útan	utan	out-travel
váðaverk	voðaverk	accident
váðaverk	voðaverk	an-accident
Valería	Vateri	Sutri (place)
vápn	vopn	weapon
vápn	vopn	weapons
vápnaskiftum	vopnaskipti	weapons-exchange
var	varð	was
várir	vorir	our
váru	voru	were
vegit	vegið	killed
verðr	verður	become
verðr	verður	worth
verit	verið	been
vetrinn	veturinn	winter
vig	víg	killing
vigit	vígið	the-killing
vígkœnn	vígkænn	battle-cunning
vilda	vildi	will
vilda	vildi	wish
vilit	viljið	wish
visar	vísar	saw
vit	við	with
yðr	ykkur	you

www.ingramcontent.com/pod-product-compliance
Lightning Source LLC
Chambersburg PA
CBHW051420070526
44584CB00023B/3519